Pueti d'Arba Sicula/Poets of Arba Sicula

Volume V: *Sicilian Erotica*

This series is intended as a showcase for Sicilian poetry. Since poetry is the best mirror of a nation's soul, these volumes offer English-speaking people an opportunity to know and understand the Sicilian people better. Two other volumes have been published:

Volume I
Vincenzo Ancona, *Malidittu la lingua/Damned language*, edited by Anna Chairetakis and Joseph Sciorra, translated into English by Gaetano Cipolla, 1990;

Volume II
The Poetry of Nino Martoglio, edited, introduced and translated by Gaetano Cipolla, 1993.

Volume III
Giovanni Meli, *Moral Fables and Other Poems*, edited, introduced and translated by Gaetano Cipolla, 1995.

Volume IV
Antonino Provenzano, *Vinissi/I'd Love to Come*, edited and translated into English verse by Gaetano Cipolla, 1995.

Library of Congress Cataloging-in-Publication Data

Sicilian erotica : a bilingual anthology of erotic poems / by Giovanni
    Meli, Domenico Tempio & Giuseppe Marco Calvino ; edited and
    translated into English verse by Onat Claypole ; introduction by
    Justin Vitiello.
    p. cm. — (Pueti d'Arba Sicula=Poets of Arba Sicula; 5)
    Includes bibliographical references
    ISBN 1-881901-10-6 (pbk.)
    1. Erotic poetry, Sicilian—Translations into English. 2. Sicilian
poetry—Italy—Sicily—Translations into English. I. Claypole, Onat.
II. Meli, Giovanni, 1740-1815. Selections. English & Sicilian.
III. Tempio, Domenico, 1750-1820. Selections. English & Sicilian.
IV. Calvino, Giuseppe Marco,1785-1833. Selections. English &
Sicilian. V. Series: Pueti d'Arba Sicula ; v. 5.
PQ5902.S53S58 1997
851.009'03538—dc21   96-53354
                                               CIP

Acknowledgments

Some of the poems in the Meli section, which appeared originally in *Moral Fables and Other Poems* in Gaetano Cipolla's translation, are reprinted here with permission. The editor also expresses his appreciation to Nicolò D'Alessandro for the use of his "Studio per un nudo" on the cover and of "The Kiss" on p. 5.

For information and for orders, write to:

Legas

P.O. Box 040328	P.O. Box 4, Stn A	38 Stayner Ave
Brooklyn, New York	Ottawa, Ontario	Toronto, Ontario
11204	K1N 8V1	M6B 1N6
USA	Canada	Canada

Sicilian Erotica

**A Bilingual Anthology of Erotic Poems by Giovanni Meli,
Domenico Tempio and Giuseppe Marco Calvino**

Edited and Translated into English Verse
by
ONAT CLAYPOLE

Introduction by Justin Vitiello

L E G A S

The Kiss by Nicolò D'Alessandro

Table of Contents

An Overview of Eroticism in Western Poetry:
from the Greeks to the Enlightenment

by Justin Vitiello

In 1912, Sigmund Freud identified the source of the disorder in the sexual life of socialized human beings: "the coprophilic elements in the instinct (i.e., our libidinous urges of *eros,* or love, and *thanatos,* or death, my note) have proved incompatible with our aesthetic ideas, probably since the time when man developed an upright posture and so removed his organ of smell from the ground."[1] Acknowledging that the sublimation, or repression, of our instincts is the necessary step humans have inevitably taken in progressing toward civilization, Freud thereby explains how we, constitutionally, do not have much of a capacity for true happiness, i.e., libidinous gratification without restraint. For Freud, however, this overly-civilized, and therefore neurotic, beast that we have become has some consolation for being so repressed: "The fundamental processes which promote erotic excitation remain always the same. Excremental things are all too intimately and inseparably bound up with sexual things; the position of the genital organs *inter urinas et faeces* remains the decisive and unchangeable factor. The genitals themselves have not undergone the development of the rest of the human form in the direction of beauty; they have retained their animal cast; and so even today love, too, is in essence as animal as it ever was."[2]

Notwithstanding this trace of primordial satisfaction that we experience in sex, Freud identifies a "fateful process of civilization"[3] that, via renunciation of our innermost desires "presupposes precisely the non-satisfaction of power instincts. While such sublimation makesour cultural development possible via our "higher psychical activities, scientific, artistic or ideological,"[4] Freud's view of the presumably greatest achievements and ideals of humankind is grim: "what we call our civilization is largely responsible for our misery, and ... we should be much happier if we gave it up and returned to primitive conditions."[5] Thus returning atavistically to our pristine state of nature, we would no longer, according to Freud, suffer neurotically that psychic and cultural dichotomy wherein "love comes into opposition to the interests of civilization" and "civilization threatens love with substantial restrictions."[6]

While Freud's psychoanalytic view of the evolution of the civilized human has profound implications for any study of erotic poetry (the overview of which is my task at hand), it is also crucial to see the relationship between eroticism and lyric art in an historico-cultural context. Herein Johan Huizinga's theory of humankind as first and foremost a *homo ludens*, not a *homo sapiens,* can be applied with considerable fruition.[7] Seeing human activity, i.e., all our cultural constructs as ludic, Huizinga explains *poesis* (the Greek word for creativity) as "play-function. It proceeds within the play-ground of the mind, in a world of its own which the mind creates for it ... It lies ... on that more primitive and original level where the child, the animals, the savage and the seer belong, in the region of dream, enchantment, ecstasy, laughter."[8] If Huizinga had been a psychoanalytic scholar, he would have developed an argument as antidote to Freud's pessimism: notably, that via poetic play humans can liberate their unconscious, their instincts of *Eros* and *Thanatos,* letting them flow in creative forms of cultural activity that bring us as much joy as pain, as much comedy as tragedy, as much pleasure as misery: "All poetry is born of play: the sacred play of worship, the festive play of courtship, the martial play of the contest, the disputatious play of braggadocio, mockery and invective, the nimble play of wit and readiness."[9] Certainly, then, erotic poetry can be appreciated as a kind of play that shares its origins with the birth of human culture.

In Huizinga's view, however, erotic poetry must be differentiated from what, since modern times, has been called "pornography." This Dutch scholar/thinker makes a distinction between the erotic and the "obscene" which I will eventually apply in this essay regarding Meli, Tempio and Calvino: "It is not the (sex) act as such that the spirit of language tends to conceive as play; rather the road thereto, the preparation for an introduction to 'love', which is often made enticing by all sorts of playing. This is particularly true when one of the sexes has to rouse or win the other over to copulating."[10]

Huizinga raises another issue that strikes me as germane to the history of erotic poetry I intend to map out: "How far is the play-quality of poetry preserved when civilization grows more complicated?"[11] In fact, a reading of some love, and hate, poems that we now consider "classics" will demonstrate how ancient poets dealt with foreplay, sensuality and sex in much more spontaneous, guiltless, and open ways than the moderns ever dared dream of. To bespecific, I refer to the Greeks and the Romans, for whom the moralistic categories implied by the notions of pornography, obscenity and scatology did not exist!

Anton Chekhov, in an 1887 letter to M. V. Kiselev, makes a similar point: "I do not know who is right: Homer, Shakespeare, ... the ancients who did not fear to grub in the 'dung-hill', but who were more stable in their moral relations than we; or the modern writers, fastidious on paper, but coldly cynical in soul and in their manner of life? I do not know who has bad taste: the Greeks, who were not ashamed to sing such love as really is in beautiful Nature, or the readers of Gaboriau, Marlitt, Per Bobo" (nineteenth century writers of "pulp fiction," my note).[12]

Keeping such distinctions in mind, let us proceed to the Greeks and Romans, and a few Italians, most of them canonical authors, who "sing such love" (and hate) without the guilt-ridden, hypocritical, or pseudo-moral codes Petronius (d. 66) satirizes in the following poem from his classic *The Satyricon,* where he asserts that "nothing is falser than people's preconceptions and ready-made opinions; nothing is sillier than their sham morality":[13]

Then why in heaven's name
must every nagging prude
of Cato's ilk cry shame,
denounce my work as lewd,
damning with a look
my guileless, simple art,
this simple, modern book?
To prudes I now assert
my purity of speech;
such candor in my pen
as will not stoop to teach.
I write of living men,

the things they say and do,
of every human act
admitted to be true. (p. 164)

Clearly, Sappho (7th-6th century B.C.E.) had no qualms about lyricizing how she and the young women she loved experienced sheer erotic delight, and agony, without a trace of self-consciousness or what we erroneously call in an era informed by Judaeo-Christian values "original sin":[14]

To me he looks godlike . . .
listening closely to the murmur of
your sweet words
and lovely laugh; my heart quivers
in my chest. Now, just
looking at you, I have
no voice left,
my tongue is broken, and an airy flame
runs clean through me . . .

sweat pours down me, and my body
shudders . . .[15]

Virtually orgasmic while watching her lover (the woman, not the man), Sappho incarnates a pure, ineffable passion in the most corporeal of images, living her pain as if Pandora's Box had never been opened. In Sappho, sacred and profane love (*eros*) are one in a kind of Golden Age Freud might have heralded as a return to "primitive conditions" of happiness where sensuality is genderless and uninhibited and where what we would call voyeurism is a pristine celebration of the libido.

While Catullus (87-54 B.C.E.) is more conscious than Sappho of what gender-directed and properly-matched genital love might be (in fact, he "translated" her poem "To me he looks godlike," making it a heterosexual love-triangle), his sense of play might be considered unbridled in modern terms. But our civilization was still relatively young and not so complicated by distinctions between what Augustine called *caritas* (true love directed to God), *cupiditas* (lust, i.e., love focussed on other creatures) and *bestialitas*. While "making love" with animals is

12

relegated in modern times to hard-porno flicks, in Catullus it is, to recall Huizinga, "made enticing by all sorts of playing":

> Lesbia's sparrow!
> Lesbia's plaything!
> in her lap or at her breast
> when Catullus's desire
> gleams
> and fancies playing at something . . .
> you are invited to nip her finger
> you are coaxed into pecking sharply,
> if I could play with you . . . [16]

Ovid (43 B.C.E.-ca. 18 C.E.), among the classics, is the poet whomost self-consciously toys with conventional morality, teases the prudes out of their smugness, titillates prigs and libertines alike. In his poems, seduction is sheer ludic art and art is ludic seduction. Intrinsically, he seduces his prey, extrinsically his readers. But it is all in the game of Epicurus, "old master of truth,/who held that all are led/by their senses to the goal,/life-perfecting Pleasure":

> . . . Corinna entered, with her gown
> Loosened a little, and on either side
> Of her white neck the dark hair hanging down . . .
> No need for catalogue, to itemize...
> Naked, I took her, naked, till we lay
> Worn out, done in. Grant me, O gods, the boon
> Of many such another sultry noon! [17]

One might think, ingenuously or hypocritically, that in the transition from "pagan" to Christian civilizations that this non-neurotic enjoyment of sex, a guiltless interplay of the sacred and the profane, would change rapidly and radically. On the contrary, from the Paleo-Christian period to the Late Middle Ages, and even into the Early Renaissance, the following observation made by Huizinga rang true as to major works of poetry and art: "The excesses and abuses resulting from an extreme familiarity with things holy, as well as the insolent mingling of pleasure with religion, are generally characteristic of periods of unshaken faith and of a deeply religious culture." [18]

While space here does not permit doing justice to an elaboration on this subtle point, I will focus on a few typical examples of the ludic interweaving of the secular and the religious wherein poets still employ what will come to be called blasphemy, obscenity, or, at least, shocking language in ways that are still closer to Sappho than to the Marquis de Sade.

My seminal text in this excursus is a Sicilian masterpiece of medieval literature: Ciullo/Cielo d'Alcamo's *Contrasto*. (Transl. my own). The poet, probably a *cantastorie* or jongleur (minstrel) displays to perfection that ludic sense of what Huizinga called "The festive play of courtship, the martial play of the contest, the disputatious play of braggadocio ..., the nimble play of wit and readiness" in a seduction poem where the young man and woman seem to be in tacit agreement that, juggling images of blasphemy, scandal and defiance, they can flaunt the religious and moral taboos of their society and have a wild verbal time in foreplay before they hop into bed. From the outset, their language is informed by eroticism:

> She: . . . you wont have me for all the world.
> First, I'd shave my head bald.
> He: If your crown's cropped, I'd rather die.
> All my relief and sport would go dry.

The shaving of the hair, a gesture of renunciation of one of the most sensual parts of a woman's body, is countered by his veiled threat to have so many orgasms (deaths) that his bucket will remain empty. Her hair, however, is such a lure to catch her fish (a risque reference to Christ and the phallus) that she reiterates the image of shorning eight stanzas later:

> I'd fall from on high if you were my fate . . .
> I'd lop all the tresses from my pate
> and be a sister in the Lord's abode
> before you could harrow my road.

To go one up on her, he takes a new path that anticipates Boccaccio's and Aretino's visions of nunneries:

> If so, Lady of Illustrious Brow,
> I'd hie to be a brother somehow,

cast my die and conquer, yes, I vow
to tarry with you at vespers and matins
and have you under my sway, in Latin.

Need one comment further on the playful blasphemy embodied in all the sexual nuances of this mock-clerical language? It is the key to the pleasure we imagine the lovers having as they provoke each other. But the plot sickens, so to speak, when she, always coyly, threatens to jump in the sea and drown herself. Once again, he rises to the occasion:

Dive, Lady so courtly and fine,
I'll paddle along through the brine
and when you drown make you mine
for this sandy treasure to rake in:
the golden coupling with you in sin.
And feigning indignation, she is almost his:
. . . my ears've never borne such spew!
When a woman's dead from head to heal
there's no relish, comeliness, zeal.

The delightful deed is almost done, but she wants to see him squirm a bit more: "Rise, off, tomorrow we start." One suspects they have already been lying together and doing some light petting, for, as he rejoinders, "my soul's flue's at its bitter end." The Sicilian "arma" here conveys a double entendre "in sutilitate" that is difficult to render in an English translation. "Arma" is a wicked pun on soul/arm, i.e., weapon which in this case is "pointed." The *point,* I hope, is finally clear when he says "my soul's on pins and needles, aquake."

If one might want to counterargue that this erotic interplay of the sacred and the profane is a minor phenomenon in the Middle Ages, I would interpose with an example from the "Divine Poet" of that period. Dante's *Rime petrose* are rife with this kind of eroticism, especially "Col mio parlar voglio esser aspro" ("with my tongue I want to be as jagged" trans. my own). Dante's imagery throughout this poem is violent, his psychic experience agonizing, his vision of erotic play aggressive (Love is war?).

On behalf of the Lady who rejects the poet due to her "nature stony, raw and crude" the God of Love assails Dante:

> He's stampeded over me and now hovers
> with that sword that fulfilled Dido's dreams . . .

Is Dante contemplating frustrated-love-suicide? Surely he is suffering from a castration complex. But, ultimately, martyr for love, Dante envisions his revenge against his tormentress with violent eroticism:

> If I could seize those lovely tresses,
> now for me the whip and the switch,
> before tierce hitched
> together, we'd spend Vespers and Hail Mary

Clearly, this reference to the spiritual exercises of canonical prayers is sexual, in a shocking way. But Dante was never squeamish when he used language appropriate to the feelings he wanted to express.

Into the fifteenth century, this lack of inhibition regarding the use of appropriate language whether it was erotic or even scatological prevailed.

Lorenzo il Magnifico penned this carnivalesque song, the celebration of a Bacchic orgy among nymphs and satyrs (Florentine nobles?). The fleshly rite is no less joyful for the participation of the grotesque Silenus, source of guileless and guiltless mirth:

> Joyful little satyrs
> with these nymphs in love
> in woods and caves patter
> ambushing below, above...
> Dragging comes this chunk,
> Silenus on his ass,
> decrepit, joyful, drunk,
> a replete carnal mass
> no more erect for lass
> his laughter ever vast (trans. J.V.).

Perhaps it is puzzling that in the passionately Christian Middle Ages those dichotomies of Western thought that had emerged with Plato and been reinforced in the teachings of the Church Fathers did not lead to the evolution of clear aesthetic and ethical notions of obscenity and pornography in art. But as Lynn Hunt has amply demonstrated in the first chapter of the series of essays he edited, *The Invention of Pornography: Obscenity and the Origins of Modernity, 1500-1800* (New York: Zone Books, 1993), these concepts surface as part of the West's historical consciousness/conscience in that Modern World born in the High Renaissance and reaching its maturity during the Enlightenment. I will elaborate on this crucial process of the shaping of our contemporary values regarding erotism, obscenity, pornography, scatology, and the sublimation that characterizes, so we think, the Higher Arts by (1) defining the terms as we understand them today; (2) providing a sketch of key developments regarding these concepts in the history of Western poetry and culture between 1500 and 1800.

The *Oxford English Dictionary* defines "erotic" as follows: "Of or pertaining to the passion of love; concerned with or treating of love; amatory." By implication, we are talking of sexual love (in the original Greek *eros*, the meaning of ever-reaching unquenchable desire is implied). Furthermore, according to the *OED*, "erotism" means "sexual excitement." If so, by a logical step, can we say that erotic poetry excites sexually? And if this is true, given the current legal definition of pornography as a visual or written work designed to inspire "prurient" desires in viewer or reader, then where is the line drawn between sublime, or at least, wholesome love poetry, erotic literature and soft and hardcore porno?

The distinctions become clearer perhaps, when we look at the *OED*'s definitions of "obscenity": "impurity, indecency, lewdness" especially regarding "the use of language." In fact in the plural, "obscenities" denote "dirty words" or matters not discussed or carried out "decently" in public which may, on the other hand, be indulged in privately.

We must query further: what is pornography? And according to whom? The earliest known definition, says the *OED*, comes from the 1857 *Dunglison Medical Dictionary:* "a description of prostitutes or of prostitution, as a matter of public hygiene." That depiction, of course, also includes the behavior of their clients or patrons; hence "the expression or suggestion of obscene or unchaste subjects in literature or art."

Seven years later, the Webster Dictionary elaborated on the notion of pornography in art, defining it as "licentious painting employed to decorate the walls of rooms *sacred* (*sic!*) to bacchanalian orgies, examples of which exist in Pompeii." But Webster fails to note, or does not realize, that the Ancients did not see their sacred rituals, or even their paid sex practices, as pornographic! Whether performed publically or privately, they were expressions of erotism. Recall Chekhov, *in re* what is "really is in beautiful Nature." It took us Moderns to judge as dirty the free and paid sexual practices of people of all persuasions and to relegate "orgies" to the realm of the obscene and the perverse. Strange for a society that deems itself the epitome of tolerance.

Scatology is another term charged with the ambivalence of a dichotomized culture. On the one hand, according to the *OED*, it is a "branch of science which deals with diagnosis by means of the faeces" and a crucial tool of analysis in paleontology. On the other hand, it denotes "filthy literature." We will see how, in poets like Michelangelo, Quevedo and Swift, this ambivalence takes on monstrous, and paranoid proportions.

We come to sublimation, our final key concept in this excursus on eroticism which, by the way, is defined in the 1988 Random House College Dictionary as "the sexual ... quality or character of something, . . . the use of sexually arousing symbolism, ... sexual drive or tendency, esp. that which is abnormal." X-rated? As erotism's opposite (and bourgeoise cure-all?), sublimation is "elevation to a higher state or plane of existence; transmutation into something higher, purer" (*OED*). Furthermore, the *OED* continues, "sublime" means "standing high above others (in attributes, feelings, actions) by reason of nobility or grandeur of nature or character; of high intellectual, moral or spiritual level." And this quality, the canons of Western aesthetics assert, is the goal of True and Beautiful Art.

But let us remember Freud who insists that it is this very sublimation that makes us unhappy. Moreover, Norman O.

Brown, drills home the idea that only by being "polymorphously perverse" in our daily lives and cultural activities can we be truly fulfilled. Does he mean we should experience life and art as orgiastic in the pagan sense? Surely, he cannot be proposing such libidinous anarchy! Cultures, societies, nations cannot function like bacchic rituals! If eroticism were to be unleashed, it would negate civilization (with or without its discontents) and its sacred cows like art, poetry, literature?

Let us return to the "invention of pornography." Hunt puts into historical, and political perspective all the issues I have just raised. I quote him here at length since his remarks are a preface to the rest of my analysis:

If we take pornography to be the explicit depiction of sexual organs and sexual practices with the aim of arousing sexual feelings, then pornography was almost always an adjunct to something else until the middle or end of the eighteenth century. In early modern Europe, that is, between 1500 and 1800, pornography was most often a vehicle for using the shock of sex to criticize religious and political authorities.... Although desire, sensuality, eroticism and even the explicit depiction of sexual organs can be found in many, if not all, times and places, pornography as a legal and artistic category seems to be an especially Western idea with a specific chronology and geography. (pp. 10-11)

Perhaps the first, consciously pornographic writer in this context, according to Hunt, was the Italian, Pietro Aretino (1492-1556). His *Ragionamenti* (1534-1536), a bawdy and satirical dialogue between a mature, well-travelled woman and an inexperienced girl, became the "model" for the pornographic European literature culminating in the Marquis de Sade's *La Philosophie dans le boudoir* (1795). In the Italian text, via the voice of the prostitute Antonia, Aretino flaunts his no-hypocritical-nonsense attitude: "Speak plainly and say 'fuck,' 'prick,' 'cunt' and 'ass.'"[19] One of Aretino's epistles makes explicit his deliberate and viciously witty attack on the prevailing moral and social taboos established by corrupt religious and political authorities: "I renounce the bad judgment and dirty habit which forbids the eyes to see what pleases them most ... It seems to me that the you-know-what given us by nature for the preservation of the species should be worn as a pendant round our necks or as a badge in our caps, since it is the spring that pours out the flood of humanity."[20] He thus links the major features that will characterize the pornographic tradition: "the explicit representation of sexual activity, ...the discussion of the behavior of prostitutes and the challenge to moral conventions of the day."[21]

This tradition will subsequently develop in a direction to be taken by the likes of Michelangelo, the courtesan Veronica Franco, Francisco de Quevedo, and two of the poets present in this volume: Tempio and Calvino. The trend is aptly summarized by Hunt, in reference to one of the essays in his book:

In her essay on the obscene word, Lucienne Frappier-Mazur explores the significance of the language of transgression. The obscene word played on the contrast between different social registers of language crude and elegant, lower and upper class, masculine and feminine in order to achieve its effect. To enact social transgression and a kind of hyperrealism, obscene language fetishizes certain words related to sex; the obscene word substitutes for the body part in question but, in the process, acquires the status of a fetish. As a consequence, the original emphasis on realism paradoxically devolves into a form of the grotesque, where penises are always huge, vaginas multiply in number and sexual coupling takes place in a kind of frenzy that is hardly 'realistic.' (pp. 37-38).[22]

Influenced by his friend Francesco Berni (1497-1535), whose scatological poetry reached its peak in "Ode to a Urinal," Michelangelo (1475-1564) launches into a Bernesque *capitolo* in *terza rima,* a self-caricature where he appears grotesque, monstrous, yet divine:[23]

> I am shut up here, all alone and poor
> as is the pulp of a fruit by its husk . . .
> Around my doorway I find gigantic dung-heaps,
> as if nobody who eats grapes, or has taken
> a physic, ever goes anywhere else to shit.[24]

With a veiled satirical reference to Julius II and the corruption of the Pope's court, the source of the poet's moral outrage, personal frustrations, and the s__ he had to take from his overbearing and unbearable patron, Michelangelo proceeds to a lamentation on his maladies that reeks of hyperrealism and anal fetichism:

> My soul is so much better off than my body
> that if, once unstopped, my body let out its stink,
> not even bread and cheese could hold the soul in[25]

Yet, as grotesque as he views himself ("My face has a shape that's enough to terrify"), he raises his gargoyle form to the stature of a deity: "I've got a bumblebee inside my jug."[26] Actually, the Italian reads "calabron" not bumblebee, but hornet, an insect that, given the iconography of the times, evoked the image of Silenus, that lewdest of Satyrs who, one day greedily looking for honey, found a hornets' nest and was badly bitten for his troubles. Thus Michelangelo represents himself as hideous but immortal, gross but divine, slimey but sublime. Finally, in the poem, he becomes, no matter how sullied, a virtual Christ:

> Whoever saw me would say I'm right for a part
> in the Magi's Feast . . .
> what good was my wish to make so many playthings,
> if they've brought me to the same end as that man
> who crossed the sea only to drown in snot?[27]

Down-playing his art that gave him the nickname "Divine Angel," this mock self-portrait incorporates obscene, crude words, as well as lofty and pure ones, to represent the poet's serious eschatological concerns (salvation, especially) via scatology.

While she does not indulge in the shocking use of "profanities," the Venetian court prostitute Veronica Franco (1546-1591) makes a fetish of her body, its allurements, and its sexual dexterity. While her language is quite elegant and informed with classical imagery, her import ranges from the subtlety titillating to the boldly provocative:

> I become so delectable, so sweet,
> sleeping with one who makes me feel right,
> welcome, loved, and sheltered under the sheet

where that sport of mine surpasses all delight . . .
I, well-trained for such arts and ruses,
create in bed, so that Apollo's arts[28]
leave a bit desired compared to my muses. (trans. J.V.)

Here we have a case unlike that typical literary device in pornography whereby writers like Aretino or Sade in *Justine* invent female narrators to set up "structures of voyeurism and eavesdropping ... , which turn the male readers of such works into complicit third parties."[29] Instead, we get a peek into the boudoir straight from the porno-whore's mouth.

The modern Argentine writer Jorge Luis Borges had this to say about Quevedo (1580-1645): "he continues to be the foremost artificer in Hispanic letters. Like Joyce, Goethe,Shakespeare, Dante like no other writer Francisco de Quevedo is, rather than a man, an extensive and complex literature."[30] I will, however, focus on Quevedo's virulent streak of obscenity which manifests itself in a monstrous verbal energy and a demonic vision of womankind, sex and sexual paraphernalia. These sonnets, all taken from his *Satires and Burlesques,* defy academic description. Their imagery ranges from nasty satire, to surreal pornography, or just plain filth. One almost forgets the sexual and scatological aspects of the poems and might marvel at the rage that spews from the poet's very being. Perhaps it is of avail here to quote three sonnets in part. First, the least obscene, "A woman in petticoats with a sharp-painted nose," mitigated with some subtlety bawdy lines and satirical barbs hurled at the authorities:

If you're a bell, where the hell's the bell-clap?...
if wedding cake, I'd like a nice piece wrapped...
If Inquisitor's hood, shove yourself up his ass!
and if a woman, with those skirts go straight to hell.[31]

The misogyny permeating Quevedo's poems reaches its peak of gruesome reification of womankind and of the frenzy of revolting sexuality in the following sonnet:

Thorny in your habits and in your face,
you could be lovely among the toads

if you had warts and learned their pissing codes,
you paragon of measles a devil wouldnt chase.
The stains on your mug were surely flung from hell;
what's blonde's not the sun but your gaping gorge,
and your face is gravy that from a sieve still hangs.[32]

Finally, Quevedo outdoes himself in this scathing, scatological, loathsome parody of sublime verses to the mock-courtly Lady who shines eternally as the Noble Poet's sun:

Oh bright red sun, to whom I've often sung,
your only eye is a gaping asshole
and a ring of keys, and the pupil black as coal
is a solid steaming pile of dung...
Your shit is shit and your piss is piss,
the one dark maze, the other a spring from the heart
and in the privy is where we find true bliss.[33]

When we look at N. O. Brown's chapter in *Life Against Death,* "The Excremental Vision," where he provides a provocative analysis of the scatological poetry of Jonathan Swift, we might reflect back on Quevedo's work and discover its "redeeming value." Brown says of Swift: "Any reader of Jonathan Swift knows that in his analysis of human nature there is an emphasis on, and attitude toward, the anal function that is unique in Western literature. In mere quantity of scatological imagery he may be equaled by Rabelais and Aristophanes; but whereas for Rabelais and Aristophanes the anal function is a part of the total human being which they make us love because it is a part of life, for Swift it becomes the decisive weapon in his assault on the pretensions, the pride, even the self-respect of mankind" (p. 179). Brown's subsequent reading of three Swiftian satiric poems *The Lady's Dressing Room, Strephon and Chloe,* and *Cassinus and Peter* zooms in one theme: that the Sublime Lady, object of the highest kind of love, to the scandalous, traumatic shock of the delicate spirits of Lofty Beaus, does something atrocious that rhymes with "wits" and "fits" (and even almost with spirits):

Oh! Caelia, Caelia, Caelia... .

Swift, argues Brown, is undercutting sublime ideals of the Enlightenment that championed lofty, rational love to the detriment of the "lower" functions of the body, i.e., the fulfillment longed for by a repressed, polymorphously perverse human psyche. Exposing these sacred values of a rationalist civilization as illusions based on repression of real *eros*, Swift, with a biting wit as sharp as a scientific dissection, roots his poetic discourse in what Brown calls "the conflict between our animal body, appropriately epitomized in the anal function, and our pretentious sublimations, more specifically the pretensions of sublimated or romantic-Platonic love" (p. 186). Thus, when "the excremental function of the beloved" (pp. 186-87) is revealed inadvertently to the Platonic lovers in these three poems, they experience a crisis, a virtual psychic breakdown. Reason is a fig here! So laments Cassinus, in deep trauma:

> Nor wonder how I lost my wits;
> Oh! Caelia, Caelia, Caelia sh____.[34]

For Swift then, according to Brown, "the extensive role of anal erotism in the formation of human culture" (p. 191) must be acknowledged. As the poet writes in *The Lady's Dressing Room* (1730):

> Should I the Queen of Love refuse
> Because she rose from stinking Ooze?[35]

Is Swift then saying that a healthy civilization will not repress anality and will not base its ethical and aesthetic values on repression of all forms of erotism?:

> Such Order from Confusion sprung,
> Such gaudy Tulips rais'd from Dung.[36]

In short, is Swift asking very disturbing questions: i.e., what's wrong with pornography, obscenity, scatology? Are they parts of our nature to be exploited in our artistic and scientific forms of cultural expression? Maybe we should really emulate the ancients, as Chekhov would have had us do?

These issues would come to a head around the period of the French Revolution when Sade vented his spleen against the hypocrisies of Western civilization and asserted the triumph of polymorphous perversity, coprophilia, sheer libidinous urges, and what Freud termed "the sadistic elements belonging to the erotic instinct." Less verbally dexterous than Quevedo, Sade (1740-1814) embodied in his works notably, *The 120 Days and Nights of Sodom* (1782-85), *Justine, Or the Misadventures of Virtue* (1791), *The Philosophy of the Bedroom* (1795) and *The History of Juliette* (1797) all the subversive aspects of pornography in its political, social and sexual undermining of civilization. More than any other pioneer in the history of the id's revolution a role that earned him 30 years in prison, Sade epitomized the essence of pornography as it had assumed its identity by the middle of the seventeenth century: "the self-conscious aim of arousing sexual desire in the reader, the juxtaposition of the material truth of sex against the hypocritical conventions of society and the rulings of the church, and . . . the cataloging of 'perversions' as so many variations on a self-justified, amoral gratification of the senses (even when some of these perversions were supposedly condemned). These aspects, as well as the emergence of libertinism as a mode of thought and action (my note: Giacomo Casanova will soon enter on the European scene), were related to the new emphasis on the value of nature and the sense as sources of authority. From the beginning pornography had close ties to the new science as well as to political criticism."[37]

While we are still agonizing, in our cultural polemics, over erotism, obscenity and pornography precisely in the above terms, I will resist entering the list and, instead, turn to my final agon: the contextualizing of the three Sicilian poets translated by Claypole in my overview of Western love and/or sex poetry. We will see that only Meli eschews pornography in his love poems and socio-political satires, thus exemplifying Huizinga's notions of ludism: "It is not the (sex) act as such that the spirit of language tends to conceive as play; rather the road thereto, the preparation for and introduction to 'love,' which is . . . made enticing by all sorts of playing." In contrast, Tempio and Calvino both take porno-poetic license in their works, conceivably because of a liberalized cultural atmosphere in the Kingdom of the Two Sicilies ruled by the Spanish viceroys toward the end of the eighteenth century: "With the Inquisition abolished and the Society of Jesus (the Jesuits) temporarily eliminated, Viceroy Caracciolo was able to suspend literary censorship and to introduce some Enlightenment reforms."[38] This approach did in fact, bring on the backlash of condemnation by the society, whereas Meli, much more subtle in his role as gadfly, was never doubted for his high moral stand: "When arts and letters were employed to illustrate and denounce a reality wherein most people were oppressed and the authorities hypocritically ignored their condition, poets, like Tempio, who deployed erotism as social critique were judged to be obscene, whereas poets, like Meli, who simply mirrored this reality by yielding to its apparently absolute and preconstituted principles were considered moralists."[39]

Giovanni Meli[40] (1740-1815), born in Palermo, came from an artisan family, but his father Antonio, a goldsmith, gave him an elitist Jesuit education. Rebelling at least privately against this dogmatic training, at 16 he began to educate himself in the Latin and Italian classics and the French Encyclopedists (Diderot, d'Alembert, Montesquieu, Voltaire, Rousseau, *et al.*). Shortly thereafter his mother convinced him to study medicine at the University of Palermo. While he would receive his degree *ad honorem* only in 1808 (seven years before his death),[41] he was thus exposed to the most prominent physicians of the age. At the same time, he began to pen verses, influenced by Arcadians like Metastasio, Rolli and Frugoni. From this literary contact, there emerged the first of his important books of poetry, *La Fata Galanti* (1761-62) and, after being named medical officer of Cinisi (30 kms. from Palermo), *La Buccolica* (1762-72). It was also during this period (1762-67) that he wrote *The Origin of the World* (1768-1770) though it was only published in 1787.[42] Apropos of these poems, Cipolla identifies the major traits of Meli's entire *opus:* "his penchant for philosophical and literary satire, his concern for social problems, his personal aspiration for a life of peace and tranquility in the bosom of mother nature, and his vocation as a painter of idyllic and bucolic scenes."[43]

Back in Palermo in 1767 to take over the medical practice of a certain Dr. Gianconte, Meli embarked on what Cipolla calls "the happiest season" of his life. For there "dawned a period of great success: loves, honor and money were his to enjoy. Already famous, Meli became the favorite of the Palermitan aristocracy. The ladies of the nobility vied to have him as a guest at their elegant parties."[44] It is precisely at this juncture that he wrote most, if not all, of the poems translated by Claypole in this collection. Rooted in the love poetry tradition of the Sicilian School and the Arcadia, Meli, according to Cipolla, is simultaneously original and genial as an erotic *vates:* "His consummate artistry and absolute command of his linguistic medium contributed to the creation of the most delicate, erotic odes of his time. In a rarefied atmosphere of sighs and restrained sensuality, of words that are whispered, the poet celebrated various parts of the beloved's figure."[45]

While readers can enjoy for themselves the sensuous language and urbane wit of such poems in this present volume as "The Lips," "The Hair," "The Voice," "The Mouth," "The Eyes," I find it sufficient to quote from just one, "The Beauty Mark" (p. 27). Echoing the playfulness of a composite Catullus/Ciullo d'Alcamo, Meli refines his eroticism via coy conceits. *Eros* is sublimated in this rarefied aristocratic milieu, but the play, on the up-and-up, is clearly sexual:

> Beauty mark, you are blessed!
> (or are you a little mole?),
> who dwell on so sweet a breast!
> if I too could share your role!
>
> In such untrammeled snow
> how you glisten, how you fit.
> This poor heart is beating so
> how my taste buds longs for it!

Rarely does Meli, in his erotic juggling of the sacred and the profane, the elegant and the earthy, resort to "four letter words." But it is significant that he does so in a political satire, "Against the Abbot Ricca" (p. 49), aimed at a figurehead of the Powers-That-Were. While the attack is veiled as a mock-classical epigram, it is levelled on the "minchioni" of the corrupt Church and State:

> The cyclops Polyphemus, with Acis gone,
> screwed Galathea every night and day
> and out of soreness for his marathon,
> he got a blister on his pizza pie.
> The surgeon cut him open and what came
> out of his cock? A real portentous sight!
> A very little man, Ricca by name,
> who can be called a dickhead by birthright!

In his introduction to *Poeti erotici del '700 italiano* (see note 52), Luigi Tassoni sheds light on why we have no evidence of the persecution of erotic and satiric poets during that period. According to Tassoni, poets of the eighteenth century lived a double life. On the one hand, in public, they dealt with the conventional subjects expected by that "enlightened society." On the other hand, in private, they penned political and literary satire and erotic and even pornographic verse. Furthermore, the flaunting of the artistic, political and religious authorities was relegated to poems they rarely published in their lifetime.[46]

Such seems to be the case regarding Domenico Tempio (1750-1821). Known throughout his life as a "disturbing, even embarrassing poet" (Tassoni, p. 226) for his Enlightened Jacobine, Massonic and Democratic tendencies, Tempio wrote in the vein of oral, folk tradition. While his non-controversial works plays, satires, poems were published as *Opere* seven years before his death, his *canti erotici* were only issued posthumously in 1848.[47]

Tempio's cacophonous music transmits major strains I have delineated throughout my introduction. As Vincenzo Di Maria explains,[48] poets like Tempio straddle the fence between (1) an erotism that has literary and artistic (redeeming?) value vis-à-vis its liberation of the individual consciousness from the hypocritical constraints of bourgeoise morality and social conformism and (2) an indulgence in pornography that, arousing human beings and dehumanizing their sexuality, winds up, even if there is a satiric intention, by alienating, frustrating, and degrading the individual, especially if a "she." Let us, however, look directly at some key passages of Tempio's poetry to appreciate his satire, hyperrealism and grotesquery for what it is worth.

The Creation of the World seems to enflesh Aretino's view that one should call bread bread and wine wine. It is certainly a profanation of the sacred. But it is perhaps no more obscene that the dearly departed Inquisition, that pious Auschwitz for "unbelievers":

> When the Eternal Father raised his arm,
> having the world created in a flash,
> he made man with an ass and with a cock,
> and woman with a pussy and an ass.
> But on her anus God then put a lock
> and wrote these words so everyone could see:
> "This morsel I reserve for priestly use.
> Adam, beware! Do not attempt abuse!"

Forbidden fruit? Do what I say, not what I do? Whatever the "divine hype," humans are thrilled by breaking taboos (even if not conscious in the unleashing of their anal erotism). Is this the original sin, asks Tempio with tongue in cheek?:

> Thus Adam, who was resting on one knee,
> first took her anus's virginity.

After all, it is fun to watch, implies Tempio. Is not God omniscient?:

> Almighty Father, watching all the while,
> enjoyed each moment of that wondrous fuck...

Scandalous, scabrous, outrageously impious, Tempio is also scathing here in his assault on corrupt religious authorities.

Similarly in *The Masturbation of the Gods,* Tempio, like Homer, rends the veil covering the classical gods' sexual exploits. Granted, Tempio is crude (Homer never is), but he rises to the erotic, rather than to the pornographic at his "best moments".

Venus had not yet turned fifteen years old.
The freshness of her graceful and white skin
perfectly matched her delicate young limbs.
All things in her were beautiful and sweet (p. 59).

Naturally, in Tempio, this sublimated image of an abstracted Womankind comes crashing from its pedestal when Vulcan barges into her:

That celebrated rapist grabbed his cock
and placed it in the center of her crack,
then he unleashed a mighty angry thrust,
but only managed to wedge half the head (p. 71).

But we might ask *ourselves* if we are more offended by this language or by the rape of a woman in the USA every four minutes? Which is more obscene? Certainly, the denouement of the Tempio poem is sheer libertine voyeurism recalling the wild orgies of De Sade. But, in the description of the circle jerk of the gods, I detect a Swiftian irreverence that challenges all our civilized pretentions, including Christian ones:

Then they applied saliva by the mouthfuls
and with sheer dedication and resolve,
without the least discretion or regard,
they beat their meat like devils on a rampage.

And, we should remember, medieval Christians in Europe, while not imagining their gods like the Hindu ones who are depicted on temples in bisexual and bestial orgies, loved to sing songs about Joseph, "cuckold of God." So why expect an enlightened Sicilian to be any less blasphemous?

This argument holds true, I think, for the third poet in this collection: the Trapanese Giuseppe Marco Calvino (1785-1833). A precocious and prolific writer, he made his literary debut at nine years of age and never stopped churning out tragedies, comedies, popular songs, Bernesque parodies, classical odes, orations, translations, etc., till his untimely death at forty-eight. Calvino, unlike Tempio, lived a life full of civil responsibilities and of involvement in the major literary societies of his day. Moreover, Calvino survived what Vincenzo di Maria has characterized as "the most intense period of Sicilian history."[49] In the wake of Viceroy Caracciolo's enlightened reforms, the island was rocked by the battles for a democratic constitution, the restoration of an absolutist monarchy, a national-separatist movement, Carbonari social-democratic federalism based on the Mazzinian model, and the reaction of the Church and the Bourbon royalty that restored a reactionary regime until Garibaldi, his Red Shirts and a host of Sicilian patriots would strike the crucial blow to bring on the Risorgimento's victory (1860).

Calvino, unfortunately, had died thirty-seven years before, leaving his own manifesto of disillusionment, with no holds barred. In "The Nineteenth Century" (p. 167), he had written:

> A philosophical century!
> A fucked up century indeed . . .
> talk of Enlightenment!...
> Suffice to say that in this century
> the man who wants to fuck
> is called degenerate.
> Stealing through politics
> is not a sin at all;
> selling justice for gain
> is seen as a social contract;
> slaughtering in war
> so conquerors can boast
> is power politics and glory;
> skinning poor folks alive
> is an honorable deed
> defending rights of property;
> hoodwinking a poor soul
> is called the genius of truth . . .

The very title of the work edited by di Maria (see note 64) is indicative of Calvino's poetic vision: *Lu Dimoniu e la carni: poesie epicuree contro la falsa morale di preti, sbirri, uomini politici e amministratori ladri*: "The Devil and the Flesh: Epicurean poems against the false morality of priests, police spies, politicians, and thieving administrators." Attacking the official dogma that reason and spirit should dominate the senses, Calvino launches a defense of the animal and the Epicurean (the pleasure-loving) in man. Nor did he spare the literary academies in their insistence on sublimity in art. Yet Calvino does so in such a slashing and ironic style that di Maria is convinced of the civic and aesthetic value of the poet's language, "the last outburst of a literary revolt" (p. 10). The critic insists (in my trans.): "Today we do not see Calvino as a pornographic poet, but rather as a social and satiric one related to the traditional burlesque poetic school of the sixteenth century that gave birth to our literature in the Sicilian language."[50]

Countless examples of Calvino's redeeming value could be cited from Claypole's biting translations. At random, I offer two, both targeting the intellectual elite that had sold out to the establishment. In the first, "The Fucking Philosopher" (p. 133f.), all the high-faluting words of grand Enlightenment thinkers come down to the libido undermining bourgeoise "ethics":

> There are no pretty women
> there are no ugly women
> as long as I can screw
> it matters not with who . . .

> You're noble, you're the best,
> much sweeter than the rest,
> you who give queenly fucks,
> not even for two bucks.

And in "The Masturbating Philosopher" (p. 151f.), which borders on grotesque hyperrealism, the masturbatory fantasy challenges the polite, superficial etiquette that deems, repressively, that "you should never talk about politics, religion or sex in public." Down with all taboos, including the entire construct of a deranged civilization that exalted human nature as rational!:

> No queen is queen enough,
> no woman can fight off,
> a mighty *philosophe*
> who knows how to jerk off . . .

> The Christian universe
> which bore fate's awful curse

to fuck in pain and strife
was thus made quickly rife . . .

Nature was generous:
a pair of useful hands
it gave to each of us.
That was part of the plans.

In conclusion, I want to elaborate freely on certain perceptive comments made by Di Maria[51] concerning the three poets represented in *Sicilian Erotica* and a fourth, Ignazio Scimonelli. Di Maria sees Meli, Tempio and Scimonelli as courageous pioneers in demystifying dead aesthetic canons and socio-politico-religious systems. This scholar hazards to say that as progressives, satirists and libertarians (or even libertines), they ushered in, or virtually created, a national Sicilian language by compounding the sacred and the profane, the sublime and the ludicrous, the exalted and the earthy, and by raising the obscene to artistic heights. Moreover, according to Di Maria, when Calvino came on the literary scene, with his three predecessors already "departed," it was a credit to this Trapanese that he did not fall into the trap of the sentimental, pseudo-metaphysical, escapist language of the bourgeoise salons. Instead, Calvino continued to break revolutionary ground excavated by Meli, Tempio and Scimonelli so that even obscene and apparently pornographic poetry, not to mention the erotic, embodied that humanistic struggle to liberate humans from their ignorance and presumptions, to undermine institutionalized hypocrisy and legalized violence in the name of true *Liberté, Fraternité et Egalité,* and to exorcise the bug-a-boos (taboos) repressing the mind, body and spirit. In this context beyond the pruderies and pedantries of overly fine distinctions, the poetry of these four Sicilians was revolutionary the way it should be: by singing of the individual's freedom of thought, action and imagination. In the face of Power. Was that what the 1960's pacifists (some of them poets like Bob Dylan and Joan Baez and Phil Ochs and Joni Mitchell) meant when they shouted obscenities like "make love, not war?"

Notes

1. Quoted in Norman O. Brown, *Life Against Death: The Psychoanalytical Meaning of History* (NY: Vintage, 1959), p. 187.

2. *Ibid.*, p. 187.

3. *Civilization and Its Discontents* (NY: Norton; orginal, 1930), pp.46-7.

4. *Ibid.*, p. 44

5. *Ibid.*, p. 33.

6. *Ibid.*, p.50.

7. *"Homo ludens": A Study of the Play Element in Culture* (Boston: Beacon Press, 1950).

8. *Ibid.*, p. 119.

9. *Ibid.*, p. 129.

10. *Ibid.*, p. 129.

11. *Ibid.*, p. 129.

12. "Dung-hills as Artistic Material," Letter to M. V. Kiselev (1887) in R. Ellman and C. Feidelson, Jr. eds., *The Modern Tradition* (NY: Oxford University Press, 1965), pp. 244-5.

13. William Arrowsmith, trans. (Ann Arbor: University of Michigan Press, 1959), p. 164.

14. That sin which, in spite of Augustinian teachings, was not sex but an intellectual pride akin to the Greek *hubris.*

15. In *Sappho*, trans. N. Brown (Santa Barbara: Bandanna Books, 1986) n. p.

16. *The Poems of Catullus*, trans. Peter Wigham (NY: Penguin, 1971), p. 51.

17. *Ovid*, trans. Rolfe Humphries (Bloomington: Indiana University Press, 1970), p. 21.

18. *The Waning of the Middle Ages* (NY, 1954), p. 162.

19. Quoted by Hunt, p. 37.

20. *Ibid.*

21. See Hunt, p. 26.

22. One could, of course, write tomes on the erotic, non-pornographic poetry of the Renaissance, Baroque, Neo-Classical and Romantic periods. It, in both sacred and profane traditions, abounds, even among writers who cultivated the porno-style.

23. For a more in-depth interpretation of this poem, see J. Vitiello's, "Michelangelo's Poetry: 'Enough! Or Too Much,'" *Romanische Forschungen* 102 (Fall 1990): 1-20.

24. *The Poetry of Michelangelo*, James M. Saslow, trans. (New Haven: Yale University Press, 1991), p. 452.

25. *Ibid.*, p. 452.

26. *Ibid.*, p. 453.

27. *Ibid.*, p. 453.

28. I.e., music and poetry.

29. See Hunt, p. 38.

30. Quoted in J. V., "Francisco de Quevedo: Seven Poems," *Rackham Literary Studies* (Ann Arbor, 1972), p. 23.

31. *Ibid.*, p. 27.

32. Trans. J. V. in *ES: Publicaciones del Departamento de Inglés. Universidad de Valladolid* 12 (Sept. 1982), p. 325.

33. In *Rackham Literary Studies*, p. 26.

34. Quoted by N. O. Brown, p. 189.

35. Quoted by N. O. Brown, p. 188.

36. Quoted by N. O. Brown, p. 188.

37. See Hunt, p. 30.

38. My translation of Vincenzo di Maria, ed., *Poesie inedite di Domenico Tempio, Meli, Scimonelli, Calvino e Anonimi Siciliani del '700* (Catania: Libreria Minerva Editrice, 1975), pp. 11-12.

39. *Ibid.*, p. 12.

40. For the premier studies of the poet's life and art see Cipolla's introductions to his translations of *Don Chisciotti and Sanciu Panza* (Ottawa: Canadian Society for Italia Studies, 1986) and *Moral Fables* (Ottawa: Canadian Society for Italia Studies, 1988). These are my main sources for this brief sketch of Meli's life and works. See also Giorgio Santangelo's two-volume collection, *Giovanni Meli: Opere*, (Milano: Rizzoli, 1965), and Luigi Tassoni, ed. *Poeti erotici del '700 italiano* (Milan: Mondadori, 1994).

41. See Tassoni, p. 174.

42. For the English translation of this seminal work, see G. Cipolla, *Moral Fables and Other Poems* (New York: Legas, 1996) which contains the full text of *Origini di lu munnu, Moral Fables* and an abundant selection of other poems, including one full canto of the *Don Chisciotti.*

43. See the introduction of *Don Chisciotti...*, vi.

44. *Ibid.*, xiii.

45. *Ibid.*, xiii-xiv.

46. I have, herein summarized Tassoni's key points made on pp. 5-6.

47. See di Maria, *Poesie inedite*, p. 13, and Tassoni, p. 226, for more details.

48. *Poesie inedite*, p. 10.

49. See di Maria's introduction to G. M. Calvino, *Lu dimoniu e la carni...* (Catania: Tringale Editore, 1978), p. 7-8.

50. *Ibid.*, p. 15. See also di Maria, *I poeti burleschi dal 1500 al 1650* (Catania: Tringale editore, 1978).

51. *Ibid.*, p. 9.

Giovanni Meli

Giovanni Meli

Lu Pettu

Ntra ssu pittuzzu amabili,
ortu di rosi e ciuri,
dui mazzuneddi Amuri
cu li soi manu fa.

Ci spruzza poi cu l'ali
li fiocchi di la nivi,
ntriccia li vini e scrivi:
Lu paradisu è ccà.

Ma un'importuna nuvula
m'ottenebra lu celu:
appena ntra lu velu
na spiragghiedda c'è.

Armata d'una spingula
chi pari na laparda,
modestia si lu guarda:
ch'è rigurusa, ohimè!

Un Amurinu affabili
l'ammutta a jiri a mia,
ma l'autru, oh tirannia!
turnari poi lu fa;

pietusu a li mei lagrimi,
chiddu lu spinci arreri,
ma torna poi 'nnarreri,
e sempri veni e va.

Li sguardi si sammuzzanu
ntra dda spiragghia nica,
ed idda li nutrica,
li pasci quantu pò;

The Bosom

In your delightful bosom,
—a garden full of roses—
Love with his hands discloses
two lovely little bunches.

Then with his open wings
he sprinkles them with snow,
and writes with veins that glow:
"This is our paradise."

A cloud most importune
comes to obscure my view,
luckily I can see through
a crack in the dark veil.

Armed with a little pin,
— a lance most harsh to me!—
on guard stands Modesty,
rigidly, without fail!

A kindly little Cupid
pushes it in my direction
the other — my destruction!—
makes him turn and then withdraw;

with pity for my tears
he fights off the attack
but then he goes right back
and so it comes and goes.

My glances dive headlong
into the tiny crack
which has the curious knack
to nurture them along;

idda la menti guida
a li biddizzi arcani,
nni teni vivi e sani
lu sulu aiutu so.

Si mai sintisti affettu,
o Zefiru amurusu,
lu velu suspittusu
allarga un pocu chiù;

e si lu to nun basta
alitu dilicatu,
pigghiati lu miu ciatu,
e servitinni tu.

Lu Neu

Tu felici, tu beatu,
'nzoccu sì, purrettu o neu!
Ntra ssu pettu dilicatu,
oh! putissi staricc'eu!

Ntra ssi nivi ancora intatti
comu sedi! comu spicchi!
Ah! Lu cori già mi sbatti,
fa la gula nnicchi-nnicchi.

Di lu coddu a li confini
sì na guardia vigilanti,
pri li vaghi dui furtini
di la piazza chiù impurtanti.

Ah! si mai pigghiannu a scanciu,
o pri audacia singulari,
qualchi manu fa lu granciu,
facci in terra trimari;

it leads my thoughts to where
the secret beauties hide,
it's able to provide
some hope for us somehow.

If ever you felt love,
my Zephyr, sweet and kind,
that cruel veil unbind;
move it a bit, I pray!

and if your breath lacks strength,
o delicate sweet breeze,
borrow my own breath, please,
and use it to this end.

The Beauty Mark

Beauty mark, you are so blessed!
(or are you a little mole?),
who dwell on so sweet a breast!
if I too could share your role!

And in such untrammeled snow
how you glisten, how you fit.
This poor heart is beating so,
how my taste buds longs for it!

At the endline of the neck,
ever vigilant, apprised
the two fortresses you check
that contain the noblest prize.

Oh, if ever by mistake,
or with sheer audacity,
someone's hand should slip your brake,
chase him off immediately!

ma quann'eu poi m'ammaraggiu,
e l'arbitriu mi manca,
fammi qualchi bon passaggiu:
cu l'amici vaia franca.

Li Baccanti

Li testi fumanu,
già semu cotti,
buttigghi e gotti
vegnanu ccà.

Vajanu a cancaru
sennu e giudiziu,
oggi sia viziu
la gravità.

Ntra la mestizia
li guai s'avanzanu,
sulu si scanzanu
stannu accussì:

la ciospa 'nzemmula
lu calasciuni,
vini abbuluni,
e amici 'nsì.

Fumu è la gloria,
l'amuri focu,
è un scherzu un jocu
la gioventù.

Prima chi tremula
vicchiaia arriva,
si sciali e viva
a cui pò chiù.

But if I should then get lost,
my will power being poor,
please allow me to get past.
Let it be! What are friends for?

The Bacchantes

We are well soused,
our heads are sore,
bring cups galore,
and bottles too!

To hell with wisdom
and common sense!
Let's all dispense
with seriousness.

When sadness reigns
our woes increase.
To find surcease
this is the way!

Give us a flute,
a concubine,
plenty of wine,
friends who say yes.

Love is a fire,
but glory's smoke;
a play, a joke,
our youthfulness.

Before our shaky
old age arrives,
let us contrive
to drink at will.

Proi ssa ciotula,
bedda Picciotta,
ch'iu ntra na botta
l'asciuchirò!

Comu rivugghinu
sti bianchi scumi,
vugghia ed addumi
lu cori to!

Tasta stu balsamu!
tastalu chissu,
l'amuri stissu
ccà dintra c'è.

Comu arrussicanu
ssi mascidduzzi!
Oh li labbruzzi!
Talè talè!

Scurra l'oceanu
l'Inglisi audaci,
ch'eu vogghiu in paci
starimi ccà.

Si poi lu pelagu
vinu sarria,
jeu scurriria
forsi chiù ddà.

Sinu a lu Messicu
vaja l'avaru,
cerchi ogni scaru
di lu Perù.

Ntra ciaschi e bimmali
sù li ricchizzi,
li cuntintizzi
ddà dintra sù.

My pretty maid,
hand me your bowl,
and I'll say skoal
and gulp it down.

See how the nectar
is foaming bright!
May it excite
your heart as well.

Taste this sweet nectar,
eat a bit more,
for at the core
there's love itself.

Oh how your cheeks
are blushing so!
Oh how they glow
those lips of yours!

And let the British
roam the wide sea.
I want to be
at home in peace.

But if the ocean
were really wine,
I'd cross that line.
Of this I'm certain.

let greedy men
roam far from here!
Search every pier
of far Peru.

Wine flasks and kegs
contain all joy:
there you'll enjoy
all happiness.

Morti nun curasi
d'oru o di ramu;
dunca tummamu!
buttigghi, olà!

Spittarla serii
è cosa grevia,
li jorna abbrevia,
sicchi ci fa.

Fora li trivuli;
allargu vaja
grunna e vicchiaia.
resti l'olè.

Gridi: Trinch-vaine;
fraula curtisa,
maetres francisa;
alon touché!

Tavuli e brinnisi,
amanti, amici,
fannu felici
l'umanità!

Viva lu viviri!
Viva lu jocu,
viva lu focu,
chi in pettu sta!

We do not care
when we are dead
for gold or lead.
So let's drink now.

Don't be too sober!
Such life is gray;
cuts short our days
and makes us thin.

So out with troubles,
chase woes away,
let the "olè"
keep us in cheer.

Yell *trinken wein,*
my sweet *fraulein*!
My wondrous wench,
who just speaks French.

Lovers and friends,
banquets and toasts,
make life a feast
for all mankind.

So cheers for living,
hurrah for games!
Cheers for the flames
inside our breasts!

L'occhi

Ucchiuzzi niuri
si taliati
faciti cadiri
casi e citati;

jeu, muru debuli
di petri e taiu,
cunsidiratilu
si allura caju!

Sia arti maggica,
sia naturali,
in vui risplendinu
biddizzi tali,

chi tutti 'nzemmula
cumponnu un ciarmu
capaci a smoviri
lu stissu marmu.

A' tanta grazia
ssa vavaredda,
quannu si situa
menza a vanedda,

chi, veru martiri
di lu disiu,
cadi in deliquiu
lu cori miu!

Si siti languidi,
ucchiuzzi cari,
cui ci pò reggiri?
cui ci pò stari?

The Eyes

Black loving eyes,
if you look coy,
houses and cities
you will destroy.

I'm but a wall
of stone and sand,
if I should crumble
please understand.

It may be magic
or nature's way,
but many beauties
you do array,

and all together
they form a charm
that my defenses
all but disarm.

Such winning graces
have your bright eyes
when they conspire
in playful guise

that a true martyr
from its desire
my heart so wretched
may soon expire.

If you are languid,
dear gentle eyes,
who can continue,
who can just gaze?

Mi veni un piulu,
chi m'assutterra,
l'alma si spiccica,
lu senziu sferra.

Poi cui pò esprimiri
lu vostru risu,
ucchiuzzi amabili,
s'è un paradisu?

Lu pettu s'aggita,
lu sangu vugghi,
sù tuttu spinguli,
sù tuttu agugghi.

Ma quantu lagrimi,
ucchiuzzi amati,
ma quantu spasimi
chi mi custati!

Ajàti làstima
di lu miu statu:
vaja, riditimi,
ca sù sanatu!

Such woe I suffer
it makes me groan,
gone is my reason,
my soul's undone.

Who can express,
enchanting eyes,
to show your laughter?
It's paradise.

My pressure rises
and my head spins.
I am all needles,
I am all pins.

How many tears,
beloved eyes,
must I still weep?
How many sighs?

For my sad state
to pity yield.
Come now, start smiling,
and I'll be healed!

Lu Labbru

Dimmi, dimmi, apuzza nica:
unni vai cussì matinu?
Nun c'è cima chi arrussica
di lu munti a nui vicinu;

Trema ancora, ancora luci
la ruggiada ntra li prati:
duna accura nun ti arruci
l'ali d'oru dilicati!

Li ciuriddi durmigghiusi
ntra li virdi soi buttuni
stannu ancora stritti e chiusi
cu li testi a pinnuluni.

Ma l'aluzza s'affatica!
Ma tu voli e fai caminu!
Dimmi, dimmi, apuzza nica,
unni vai cussì matinu?

Cerchi meli? E s'iddu è chissu,
chiudi l'ali e 'un ti straccari;
ti lu 'nzignu un locu fissu,
unni ài sempri chi sucari:

lu conusci lu miu amuri,
Nici mia di l'occhi beddi?
Ntra ddi labbri c'è un sapuri
na ducizza chi mai speddi;

ntra lu labbru culuritu
di lu caru amatu beni
c'è lu meli chiù squisitu:
suca, sucalu, ca veni.

The Lips

Tell me, tell me buzzing bee,
what so early do you seek?
There's no redness yet appearing
on the nearby mountain peak.

And along the field the dew
is aglow, still quivering.
Oh, take care you do not wet
your most dainty golden wing.

Pretty flowers, sleepy-eyed,
are still snug and tightly closed
in their verdant buds abiding
all with heads that droop and doze.

But your gentle wing is weary,
yet you soar, in air you streak. . .
Tell me, tell me, buzzing bee
what so early do you seek?

If it's honey you desire
fold your wings, strive no more.
I will show you one sure realm
where you'll find enough to store.

Don't you know my love,
my Nice, Nice with the lovely eyes?
On her lips such flavor rests
it's of sweetness a great prize.

On the lips incarnadine
of my own beloved Joy
there is honey most divine.
kiss them sweetly and enjoy.

Ddà cci misi lu Piaciri
lu so nidu ncilippatu,
pi adiscari, pi rapiri
ogni cori dilicatu.

A lu munnu 'un si po' dari
una sorti cchiù filici
chi vasari, chi sucari
li labbruzza a la mia Nici.

La Vucca

Ssi capiddi e biundi trizzi
sù jardini di biddizzi,
cussì vaghi, cussì rari,
chi li pari nun ci sù

Ma la vucca cu li fini
soi dintuzzi alabastrini,
trizzi d'oru, chi abbagghiati,
perdonati, è bedda chiù:

Nun lu negu, amati gigghia,
siti beddi a meravigghia;
siti beddi a signu tali
chi l'uguali nun ci sù.

Ma la vucca 'nzuccarata
quannu parra, quannu ciata,
gigghia beddi, gigghia amati,
perdonati, è bedda chiù.

Occhi, in vui fa pompa Amuri
di l'immensu so valuri,
vostri moti, vostri sguardi
ciammi e dardi d'iddu sù.

For it is right there that pleasure
hid its honey-covered nest
as to capture with this treasure
every heart of love possessed.

In the world there cannot be
a more joyful destiny
than to kiss and suck upon
the sweet lips of my own Nice.

The Mouth

Oh, those braids of golden hair
are a garden sweet and fair,
they're so beauteous and rare
none comparison will dare.

But the mouth with eburnine,
pearly teeth so neat, so fine,
Golden Braids that all outshine,
please don't mind, 'tis more divine.

My dear brows, I can't deny
you're as lovely as the sky,
you're so lovely to the eye,
all who see you simply sigh.

But the mouth's a sugar beet
when she opens it to greet,
lovely brows that love entreat,
please forgive me, 'tis more sweet.

Love has chosen you, dear eyes,
just to flaunt his greatest prize.
All your actions, all your sighs
represent his flames, his guise.

Ma la vucca, quannu duci
s apri, e modula la vuci,
occhi... Ah vui mi taliati!...
Pirdunati, 'un parru chiù.

Pirsuasiva amurusa

Dimmi, chi senti fari
cu st'onesta fintizza?
Agghiuttiti sta pizza
e 'un ci pinsari chiù.

Cridi sia puttana
'na donna chi si futti?
Distingu s'è cu tutti,
o pri venalità.

Ma s'è un giovinottu
di bona qualitati,
lu finciri onestati
è bestialità.

Ch'è mai st'onuri? Dimmi,
è regnu ntra la Francia?
E cosa chi si mancia?
Sintemulu zoccu è.

E' un pregiudiziu vanu,
chi cugghiunia la genti.
Futtemu allegramenti,
megghiu piaciri 'un c'è!

Chi vo chi ti dicissi?
Sì bedda e sì sanguta,
ma sì beccafuttuta
cu tia 'un ci si pò.

But the mouth I so adore
when her words begin to pour.
Lovely eyes, why do you stare?
Please forbear ... I'll say no more.

Persuasion to Love

What can you gain, I say,
with honesty that's fake?
Come swallow my sweet cake,
and think no more of it.

You think a girl's a whore
because you know she screws?
Depends with whom she does,
if it's for love or dough.

But if she loves a youth
possessed of quality,
her faking honesty
is sheer stupidity.

What's honor, can you say?
Is it a realm in France?
A thing you eat, by chance?
Let's hear it! Speak, I pray!

It is a prejudice
that makes a fool of you.
So let us gladly screw.
There is no greater joy!

What can I say, in sum?
You're pretty, and you're strong,
but we can't get along.
To me you're really dumb!

Un muccuneddu schittu
troppu lu vinni caru,
ch'è lapis di lu raru
lu sticchiceddu to?

Pesta, chi ti ni veni?
Ci hai a 'nchiudiri orio o pagghia?
Vaja prestu, chi già squagghia
st'afflittu meu cicì!

La gran matri natura
'nclina a lu futtisteriu,
futti lu desideriu
quannu la minchia 'un pò.

Anchi li bruti stissi,
privi d'umanitati,
sfoganu pri li strati
stu primu istintu so.

Futtinu l'elementi,
futtinu l'ervi stissi,
lu suli, ntra l'eclissi,
si futti, cui lu sa?

Dunca, tralascia, bedda,
sta tua onesta fintizza,
agghiuttiti sta pizza
e 'un ci pinsari chiù.

Your tasty little morsel
indeed bears a high price.
What is your little slice,
a wise man's lapis stone?

Damn it, what can you gain?
Can you store wheat or hay
in it? Make haste, I pray
for my poor dick's in pain.

All things in Mother Nature
incline to fucking too,
and when your dicks can't screw,
desire fucks for you.

Devoid of human senses
even an animal
gives in to instincts' call
and fucks right in the streets.

The elements all fuck,
the grass itself screws, too.
The sun, who knows, may screw
when there is an eclipse.

So then my fair, just quit
such honesty that's fake,
and swallow my sweet cake,
and think no more of it.

Lu giardinu d'amuri

Nici, si nun sì barbara
ed ami a mia mischinu,
fammi na vota trasiri
dintra ssu to jardinu.

'ntra ss'urticeddu amabili,
vasu di rosi e sciuri,
c'è acqua chi assaggiannula
astuta lu miu arduri.

La nsalatedda tennira
davanzi la tua porta,
lu ciauru mi stuzzica,
li peni mi conforta.

Chiù dintra poi si vidinu
violi e sempriviva
unni si fa la zagara,
filici cui ci arriva!

Cci su li minnulicchi,
chi smovinu la gula;
mi liviria l'angustia
na minnulicchia sula.

C'è un pedi di lumia,
fa un ciauru stupennu,
cci acchianiria tra st'arvulu
e ci staria in eternu.

Si vidinu chiantati
cu regula e misuri
li priziusi fraguli
accantu sti toi mura.

The Garden of Love

O my Nice, don't be cruel!
Don't allow your heart to harden
and permit me at least once
to come into your fair garden!

In your lovely little garden,
that with roses is replete
flows such water whose sweet taste
soothes the burning thirst and heat.

And the tender tasty salad
that is growing at your gate
my keen sense of smell excites
and my buds will surely sate.

And as I gaze farther in
violets and evergreen,
orange blossoms I see there:
blessed he who can go in!

There are almonds green and tender
that my taste buds so excite.
One sweet almond would destroy
every woe and every plight

And there is a lemon tree
on which I would surely climb
for its fragrance's heavenly.
I would stay there for all time.

Precious strawberries are there
all around next to your walls
which were planted with great care
and observance of the rules.

Nici, si nun sì barbara
e m'ami veramenti,
fammi na vota trasiri
ca nun ti toccu nenti.

L'acqui sù na delizia,
si ddocu dintra trasu
non stuzzicu, nun pizzicu,
ciauru, toccu e vasu.

Ottava

Lu multu rivirennu patri Onoriu,
ch'a la facci paria un San Macariu,
era divotu assai di San Caloriu
e fu a la Gancia multu nicissariu.
Cu lu cazzu faceva d'Aspersoriu,
cu li cugghiuna dicea lu rusariu
ed in suffraggiu di lu priatoriu
ficcava requii ntra lu tafanariu.

Contro l'abate Ricca

Mortu Aci, Polifemu ci la ficca
a Galatea nfina a li cugghiuni,
e, quadiatu, pri lu ficca e sficca,
ci uncia la pizza e si ci fa un bubbuni.
Lu chirurgu ci l'apri, e chi ni spicca
di ddà dintra? O solenni purtintuni!
Un omu nicu nicu, e chistu è Ricca,
scorcia non già, ma civu di minchiuni!

Nice, if you're not cruel
and for me you truly care
let me come inside one time!
I won't touch a thing in there!

If I manage to get in there,
-Oh the waters there are bliss!-
I won't tease, I will not tear,
I'll just smell, and touch and kiss.

Octave

The very reverend Honorius,
who had a face like St. Macarius,
was much devoted to our St. Calorius
who'd been in Gancia meritorious.
He used his cock as holy incensory,
his testicles he used as offertory,
and as a vow for souls in Purgatory,
amens drove in like a suppository.

Against the Abbot Ricca

The cyclops Polyphemus, with Acis gone,
screwed Galathea every night and day
and out of soreness for his marathon,
he got a blister on his pizza pie.
The surgeon cut him open and what came
out of his cock? A true, portentous sight!
A very little man, Ricca by name,
who can be called a dick head by birthright!

Domenico Tempio

Domenico Tempio

Protesta

Si cc'è cui pigghia scandalu
di ciò ch'iu scrivu, saccia
ch'iu di li frusti d'autru
nn'accollu in mia la taccia.

Scrivu chi fannu l'omini,
e fazzu a la morali
di lu prisenti seculu
processi criminali.

A quali signu arrivanu,
mia musa si proponi
dirvi li brutti vizii
e la corruzioni.

Chi di la culpa laidi
tantu l'aspetti sunu,
chi basta sulu pingirla
per aborrirla ognunu.

Protest

If someone's scandalized
by all the things I write,
tell him I won't accept
the blame for others' blight.

I write what mankind does.
My poetry indicts
the morals of our day.
That is what's in my sights.

The true goal of my Muse
is simply to expose
how rampant is the vice,
how deep corruption goes.

The misdeeds are so many,
so ugly, so diverse,
that painting them in verse
makes folks abhor them all.

La Creazione del Mondo

Quannu l'eternu Patri isau lu vrazzu,
doppu ca fici in un fiat lu munnu,
l'omu criau c'un culu e c'un cazzu,
e la cumpagna so c'un culu e un cunnu.
Ma a chista in culu misi un catinazzu
e chiaru poi ci scrissi ntunnu ntunnu:
"Distinu a li parrini stu muccuni.
Sta attentu, Adamu, non fari lu minchiuni".

"Dai misu in gravità", ci dissi all'omu,
curvatu, additta, si puru ti piaci
addinocchiati a quattru peri comu
appuntu fannu li bruti, lu to jaci
ficcari ci putrai tu tonnu tonnu
e futtiriti un'anca a taci maci.
Sta' attentu, sai, ti pruibisciu sulu
di buzzarari ficcanniccilla 'nculu."

Adamu comu un loccu s'arristau,
a sti paroli, tuttu spavintatu.
Ad Eva poi lu cunnu ci guardau
e vitti ch'era fattu spirlungatu.
Lu culu a lu cuntrariu ci tuccau
e vitti quantu beni era attunnatu.
Lu cazzu osserva tunnu, ed esclamannu,
dissi: "Sta bestia chi mi va scacciannu.

Si avissi fattu la minchia a lasagna,
lu patri Eternu, forsi m'astinia;
ma si ci trasi... a vogghia ca s'incagna,
chista è n'asinità, chista è pazzia;
tunnu cu tunnu bellu s'accumpagna
e c'incasedda cu gran simitria.
Chi ci traseva stu sticchiu spaccatu!
Setti jorna pinsau e l'ha sgarratu!"

The Creation of the World

When the Eternal Father raised his arm,
having the world created in a flash,
he made man with an ass and with a cock,
and woman with a pussy and an ass.
But on her anus God then put a lock
and wrote these words so everyone could see:
"This morsel I reserve for priestly use.
Adam, beware! Do not attempt abuse!"

"Regarding the position," he then said to man,
"you can bend down, or stand, or even kneel
on your four limbs, as do the animals,
and in this way proceed to stick your eel
inside her hole with shaft and balls.
You may fuck, if you wish, her thigh or cheek.
The only thing that I forbid, alas,
is this: you cannot fuck her in the ass."

Adam, on hearing this, was quite surprised.
In fact, he was amazed and also scared.
Eve's pussy he went on and scrutinized
and saw it was a long, slit-shaped affair.
But on examining her ass he found
that it was altogether nicely round;
and seeing that his cock was rounded too,
he cried out loud: "What is this fool up to?

If the Eternal Father made dicks flat,
like a lasagna, it's likely I'd abstain,
but if it fits...! It's mad, I won't buy that!
If God does not approve, let him complain!
Parts fit, round goes with round appropriately.
There's harmony of shapes and symmetry.
What can you stick in cracks so split and long?
He pondered seven days, and got it wrong!"

Eva, allura, ca donna era cumpita,
si pirsuasi di chista ragiuni;
misi lu culu a ponti a vocanzita
'ntra li natichi avennu lu minchiuni.
Di lu culu sbirginò la prima zita
lu patri Adamu misu a dinucchiuni.
Eccu, viditi, prima a buzzarari
Adamu s'insignau e poi a chiavari.

Mentri eranu 'ntra l'attu di lu briu
e mentri già lu quagghiu ci calava,
un Angilu, a cui parsi un gran schifiu
trasiri un cazzu unn' Eva cacava,
si mangiò la cucuzza e dissi a Diu
ch'Adamu ad Eva 'nculu la ficcava.
"Oh cazzu!" dissi allura siddiatu
lu patri Eternu: "Olà, sia castigatu!"

Subitu l'Arcangilu in fretta
curri c'un spitu 'nfucatu a li manu.
"Fermati... " ci gridau "aspetta aspetta,
stimpagna prestu sta minchia di l'anu.
Comu non t'abbastava la pruvvista
vulisti trasiri ancora, o prufanu,
'ntra ddu vuccuni ca Diu ha distinatu
a li ministri di lu celibatu?"

Eva, ca stava misa ad abbuccuni,
a sti paroli addivintau nna locca.
Scippasi cu li manu lu minchiuni
e lu vircocu vagnatu si tocca.
Adamu, ch'era misu addinucchiuni,
dissi, muncennu l'attisata nnocca:
"Si stu purtusu non vulia tuccatu,
di mia chi voli? L'avissi muratu".

Eve then who was a reasonable lass
became convinced God's logic had been weak
and bending made a bridge out of her ass,
feeling his heavy dick between her cheeks.
Thus Adam, who was resting on one knee,
first took her anus's virginity.
He learned to buttscrew first — by stroke of luck —
and only after learned he how to fuck.

While they were in the middle of the game
and while he was approaching ecstasy,
an angel who believed it was a shame,
to fuck Eve where she shits- A heresy!-
went up to God with utmost eagerness
and told him Adam had defiled Eve's ass.
In anger the Almighty Father said,
"Oh, shit! Let punishment fall on his head!"

So the Archangel quickly sauntered up,
bearing his red-hot weapon in his hands
and yelled at him: "Stop what you're doing! Stop!
Uncork that cock out of her ass at once!
God for your sake some goodies did provide.
Of that sweet morsel he had set aside,
for the good ministers of those who're chaste
you had, blaspheming man, to have a taste?"

But Eve who was in a supine position,
on hearing all these words was quite upset.
With her hands she pulled out his heavy cock
and then she felt her ass completely wet.
Adam who was still resting on his knees
complained as he milked his tumescent crest
"If He didn't want me to go in that hole,
he should have plugged it up or built a wall!"

Michelangilu allura rifiriu
d'Adamu ed Eva tuttu l'opiratu.
Ddocu lu Patri Eternu mbistialiu,
sintennu ch'era l'attu consumatu:
"Vinnitta iu nni vogghiu comu Diu.
Ogn'omu nascirà cu stu piccatu,
si secuta Adamu a ghiri 'nculu
sperdi lu munnu e sperdi in iddu sulu".

Ed eccu, misu supra un nuvuluni:
"Adamu, Adamu" allura lu chiamau
cu lu tremennu so forti vuciuni.
Adamu pri lu scantu assintumau
e ad Eva ci si mossi lu matruni
e lu virticchiu allura ci pigghiau
in vidiri di Diu l'alta putenza
ca fulminannu dissi sta sintenza:

"Di morti murirà lu snaturatu
omu ed espulsu di lu paradisu
mancirà pani a stentu travagghiatu,
stu buzzaruni e faccia di 'mpisu.
E la garrusa donna in ogni statu
sarà suggetta all'omu, ed è dicisu
di figghiari cu stentu e cu duluri,
sta buttana di culu senza onuri."

Sutta un zuccuni, chi cc'era mpinnata
d'erva e di frunni, si cunsaru un jazzu.
Adamu, chi non avia dimenticata
la dura liggi di lu catinazzu,
pigghia ad Eva e la metti stinnicchiata,
poi ntra lu sticchiu ci appunta lu cazzu
e tira cu na botta dritta e tunna
e lu sticchiu spaccatu ci l'attunna.

So Michaelangel went up to relate
everything Eve and Adam did: the works,
and the Eternal Father, when he heard
the misdeed had been done, just went berserk:
"As I am God, I now demand my vengeance!
Henceforth each man with this sin shall be born.
If Adam then continues to buttscrew,
the world is lost and he will be lost too."

And then, from high above a heavy cloud,
God called to Adam with a mighty voice,
"Adam, o Adam!" booming, very loud.
Poor Adam was so scared he lost his poise,
and out of fear poor Eve was near to swoon.
She started shaking, would have fallen soon,
when she saw the great power of the Lord
who with some lightning underscored his word.

"Let the perverted man experience death!
Let him be cast outside of paradise,
to eat stale bread earned by hard work and sweat,
that asshole fucker, and perverted louse!
And let that faggot woman always be
subject to man for all eternity;
let this whore without honor in her veins
deliver sons through hardships and through pains."

Under a roof of branches and of leaves
beside a stump, they made their lair with grass
and Adam who had not forgotten yet
the law that put a lock upon her ass,
took Eve and made her lie upon the ground,
and placing his dick's head upon her crack,
he gave a mighty thrust against her mound
and that slit-shaped long pussy changed to round!

Lu patri Eternu vitti sta chiavata
tuttu cuntentu comu un gran sumeri
e facennucci intantu nna risata
drittu ci lu tinia lu cannileri.
E fattu s'avirria una minata
s'avissi avutu manu, cazzu e peri.
Ma si lu patri Eternu avissi un cazzu
lu munnu non saria ntra stu mbarazzu.

La Minata di li Dei

Cui pati di sintomi e di stinnicchi
Pri non sentiri cosi stralunati,
Si 'ntuppassi lu zuccu di l'oricchi:
Non su pr'iddi sti cosi 'nzuccarati;
Ccà nui parramu di cazzi e di sticchi,
Di culi, di futtuti e di minati,
Cui non voli, non senta — parru sulu
A st'unioni di ffuttuti 'nculu.

Salvi, illustr'accademici! prisentu
Sti pochi versi ccu cori trimanti;
Omini ccu li cazzi a centu a centu,
E d'intra e fora, d'arretu e d'avanti,
Accurdatimi vui cumpatimentu;
Scusatimi si sugnu stravaganti;
Ed accurdati all'auturi impurtunu
Lu vostru largu ed apertu pirdunu.

Giovi, a cui era in aria lu carru
Comu 'ntra mari la varchitta, o scarmu,
Era a ddi tempi lu primu futtarru,
E avia la minchia chiù dura d'un marmu.
Cuntava di diamitru, si non sgarru,
Triccentu uttanta canni e menzu parmu;
Ed a Giununi ccu ddu cazzu santu
Cci l'avia fattu addivintari tantu!

Almighty Father, watching all the while,
enjoyed each moment of that wondrous fuck,
following every action with a smile,
holding a godly candle with a rakish look.
I think he probably would have jerked off,
if he had had two feet, hands and a cock.
But if Almighty Father had a dick, I guess,
the world today would not be such a mess.

The Masturbation of the Gods

Let those of you who are persnickety
put cotton in your ears so you can't hear
tales that you may regard as lunacy.
These honey covered things related here
are not for you. We'll talk of cocks and pussies,
we'll dwell on fucking, handjobs and asses.
If you don't want to hear, just leave! Buzz off!
Those taking it up the ass will be enough!

Illustrious academicians, hail!
As I recite these lines, my heart is quaking.
Men who're endowed with dicks that never fail
who drive them in and out in merry making,
do try to understand my awful plight.
Excuse of my extravagance the flight.
To this vexatious poet please extend
your pardon fully as you would a friend.

Jove, whose great chariot glided in the skies
as does a slender boat or a canoe at sea,
was the supreme great fucker in those days.
Harder than marble, his big cock would be,
spanned in diameter and not lengthwise,
three hundred eighty palms and a bit more.
Juno's vagina had been stretched so wide
by Jove's great cock that you'd have drowned inside.

Futteva a longu, e pertichi e bubbuni
Pigghiava spissu alla diavulina;
E intantu ccu ddu grossu so minchiuni
Arruzzulava figghi a minchia china:
Mircuriu, chi nasciu mentri Giununi
Cci avia 'mmiscatu camurria divina:
E in diversi occurrenzi e varii parti
Fici a Baccu, Vulcanu, Apollu e Marti

Senza purtari a Giovi ubbidienza,
Picciotti privi di boni cunsigghi
Pinzaru un ghiornu senza la licenza
Iri a mangiari 'n campagna sti figghi:
Subitu fu accurdata la scadenza;
Si affirraru nna pocu di buttigghi
Ed arrivati a lu locu signatu
'Ntra nenti fu lu pranzu priparatu.

Cuminciaru a manciari, e 'ntra un mumentu
Li buttigghi si vittiru agghiurnari;
Già dritti in pedi si mettunu a stentu;
Già li testi cumincianu a fumari;
Intantu di luntanu a passu lentu
La bellissima Veniri cumpari;
Ca nuda e sula pri li larghi strati
Va cugghiennu lu friscu pri la stati.

Non avia quindici anni; la frischizza
Di ddi carnuzzi aggraziati e ghianchi
Accumpagnava la dilicatizza.
Tuttu era in idda grazia e biddizza;
Di lu morbidu pettu e di li cianchi,
Beddi l'occhi, la vucca, e beddi l'anchi,
Beddi ddi labbra, comu dui girasi.
Bedda dda cosa unni si nesci e trasi.

And since Jove screwed with such intensity
he often got infections, crabs and nicks,
inspite of which, however, he went on
to father many children with that dick.
When Mercury was born, Juno gave Jove
a case of gonorrhea out of love.
In other times, under different stars,
Jove sired Apollo, Bacchus, Vulcan, Mars.

The children of great Jove who were most brash,
(young men all lacking judgment and good sense)
decided one fine day to have a bash,
not thinking Jove might take offense
So they arranged a date and gathered food
and brought along some bottles for the mood.
And once they got to the desired spot,
the table for their meal they quickly set.

They then began to eat and in no time
the bottles started showing light of day.
They'd drunk so much they had begun to sway
while their poor heads were fuming from the juice.
But in the distance lovely Venus came,
slowly approaching them with measured steps.
Alone and walking naked down the street,
she hoarded breezes for the summer heat.

Venus had not yet turned fifteen years old.
The freshness of her graceful and white skin
perfectly matched her delicate young limbs.
All things in her were beautiful and sweet;
From the soft bosom to the sloping waist;
wondrous her eyes, her nose and her fair thighs,
wondrous her lips, like cherries was her mouth;
wondrous that thing where you go in and out.

Tinti a pinneddu parianu li natichi,
Tunni, duri, citrigni e sapuriti;
Stavanu tutti a taliarla estatichi,
Ca muveva l'arrittu a li rimiti;
Aveva l'occhi vivuli e simpatichi,
Dd'occhi unn'era d'Amuri la riti;
Dd'occhi capaci, ccu na taliata,
Di squagghiari la nivi e la ilata.

Lu nasiddu paria cira chi adduma;
La vucca, si la guardi, tu nni spinni;
Li masciddi cchiù ghianchi di la scuma;
Drittu lu coddu aggraziatu scinni;
'Ntra lu pittuzzu poi, comu dui puma,
ianchi e tunni spurgevanu dui minni;
Li cosci soi, di lu cchiù espertu mastru,
Dui culonni perfetti di alabastru.

Dda cosa po' ntra ddi culonni amati,
La vidi, 'n forma rilivata e tunna,
E ghianca 'mmenzu a dui fardi spaccati,
Ca su' cuperti di nna manta biunna;
Dui culunneddi surgiunu a li lati
'Ntra lu menzu di vadda si profunna;
Tennira irvuzza intornu s'agghiummìra
Intatta di l'aratu e di vummìra.

Aviti vistu un cavaddu di razza
Vidennu la jumenta 'ntra lu chianu
Sbrugghiari dda terribili minchiazza,
E poi currirci supra a manu a manu?
Ccussì viditi la lussuria pazza,
La turba di li Dei, ca di luntanu
In vidiri la Dia ccu facci accisa,
Subitu a tutti la minchia cci attisa.

Her thighs seemed like a work done by a master:
shapely and round and solid like a column;
The gods all stared at her in ecstasy,
her charms could even perk a hermit's cock.
She had vivacious and inviting eyes,
but eyes in which she hid the net of love.
Even a simple glance from them, you felt,
the coldest snow and hardest ice would melt.

Her little nose seemed made of melting wax,
one glance at her sweet mouth would make you pine,
her shapely jaw was whiter than sea foam.
Her graceful neck was slender, long and straight.
There rose out of her delicate pure chest
two supple breast, all white and round like apples.
Her legs seemed chiseled by the greatest master:
two perfect columns carved from alabaster.

What of that thing between her columns pair?
You see it bulging a little, round in shape
and dazzlingly white between two cloven halves,
sweetly mantled with some golden hair;
two shapely columns rise along the sides,
and in the middle lies a little valley,
covered with tender grasses and sweet boughs,
untouched by human implements or plows.

A purebred stallion have you ever seen,
who spied a mare alone out in a meadow,
as he rolls out that awesome dick of his
and runs to stand upon her bye and bye?
Well, that is how that band of gods behaved:
as the approaching goddess came near them,
the mad desire of those eager jocks
showed in their faces and their swollen cocks.

Cci vannu tostu tutti cincu in fila
Ccu l'occhi russi e li cazzi arrittati—
Saziu agnunu non è, si non la 'nfila,
Si non pò tutta, almenu nna mitati;
Cui cci afferra lu culu, cui li pila,
Cui prucura di daricci minchiati,
Cui cci afferra li minni e lu capicchiu;
Cui cci appunta la minchia 'ntra lu sticchiu.

Chi c'è, picciotti ? Chi ssù sti cusazzi,
Ad unu ad unu idda cci dicia:
Ma chiddi peju assai di li crastazzi,
Assai di chiui truzzavanu la Dia:
Diu nni scanza di furia di cazzi!
Veniri unni guardari non sapia;
Cci arrinesci alla fini di scappari
E si metti in disparti a taliari.

Marti, ch'era smargiazzu e 'nghirriusu,
Non suleva suffriri musca a nasu;
Vaia, dicia, cc'è ccà qualchi garrusu,
Ca pritenni 'nfilari unni iu trasu ?
Niscissi fora, ca cc'è lu rifusu;
Niscissi, ca lu fazzu pirsuasu;
A futtirivi tutti bastu iu sulu,
Non sugnu Marti, si non vaju 'nculu,

Apollu rispunnia: va duna l'anchi,
Ccu sti to vapparii, tu non mi arrunchi,
Forsi cridi ca l'autri sù vanchi,
Sù locchi, sù minchiuni, sunu junchi?
Cca c'è qualchi pirsuna, ca puranchi
Si senti cori, e non ha manu ciunchi;
Chi futti comu avissi centu minchi,
Chi ti sbarra lu culu e ti lu inchi.

All five of them approached her one by one
with bloodshot eyes and dicks as hard as rocks.
And each of them would not be satisfied
until he'd plunged his dick if not all in,
at least halfway. Some grabbed her ass, her hair,
while others tried to poke her with their cocks;
one bit her nipple, one pulled at her teat,
one aimed his dick to see if it would fit.

What's all this, boys? What are these awful things?
She kept repeating to each one of them.
But all of them as though they were he-goats
kept poking at the goddess without pause.
God spare us from the fury of a dick!
Venus just did not know where she could turn.
But finally she managed to get clear,
and moved away to stare at them in fear.

Being a quarrelsome and boastful fellow,
forever itching for a fight, Mars said:
"Come on, is there someone among you fags
who thinks that he will go where I go in?
Come forth, I'll give you more than you can take!
Come on, advance and you will be convinced.
My dick is strong enough to screw you all.
My name's not Mars if Venus I don't ball!"

Apollo answered him: "Go take a walk!
This macho game you play won't scare a soul!
You think perhaps the others here are lame,
you think we're simpletons, dickheads, or fools?
There are folks here who will not hesitate,
who know well how to utilize their hands;
who screw with cocks much bigger than a bull's,
who can stretch out your ass and stuff it full!"

Lu figghiu di Semeli parsi un braccu,
Dissi: non dura a longu chistu addiccu;
Santu di Cavuluni, 'un sugnu Baccu,
Si 'ntra l'ultima crispa 'un ci la ficcu;
Non tiru avanti pirchì sugnu straccu;
Mi sentu già lu cannarozzu siccu;
Ma cazzu! Siddu viju ddu buccuni,
Cci la ficcu ccu tutti li cugghiuni.

Mircuriu rispunnia: talia cui parra!
Quali minchiunaria all'autru afferra;
Un 'mbriacu, un bunaca, un menzu-garra,
Mischinu! Non è in celu e mancu in terra:
Va cerchiti cu c'è ca ti lu sbarra;
Ca si tanticchia lu sensu mi sferra,
A sti Dii di li sensi e di la murra
Li fazzu pezzi pezzi, comu surra.

Dissi Vulcanu: va, zittu minchiuni,
Re di li primi ruffiani e latri;
Papà di l'impusturi e l'attimpuni,
Accusirissi macari a to patri.
Veniri tocca a mia, si lu spiuni
Tu non facevi a Giununi me matri;
Veniri non purtassi di la fascia
Lu titulu di figghia di bagascia.

La Fama è maldicenti ed anchi è pazza;
Sbogghia li pinni e poi lu culu appizza;
Già lu raccunta a Giovi e lu strapazza,
E ccu lu diri so l'accendi e attizza:
Lu Diu supremu subitu s'incazza,
Si metti a santiari pri la stizza;
Pinsau di poi, e tutta l'ira smorza,
D'unirsi ad iddi e a parrari s'inforza.

The son of Semele looked like a hound
and said: "This teasing won't go on much longer;
My name's not Bacchus, if I, confound it,
won't stick my dick inside each hole she has.
I will not go ahead of everyone because I'm peaked
My gullet feels already somewhat parched;
But damn it, when I see that sweet young thing,
I want to burrow into her with everything."

Mercury intervened: "Just look who's talking!
One lamebrain trying to outdo the other,
a drunkard, a half-pint and a poor fag!
He's neither on the ground nor in the sky.
Go look for someone who can spread your cheeks.
For if I really let myself get mad,
divinities of games and of the senses,
I'll grind you to a pulp and make you blintzes!"

Vulcan replied: "Go on, shut up, you jerk,
monarch of the first ruffians and thieves;
daddy of all impostors and con men.
You'd even testify against your father.
Venus belongs to me, no doubt about it.
If you had not spied on my mother Juno,
Venus today would not have had to wear
the appellation: *Daughter of a whore.*"

Fame is a wagging tongue and she is nuts,
she spreads her wings and then she pays the piper.
Already she had reached Jove's ear, upsetting him,
the more he heard the more he grew upset,
the Highest Jove quite simply lost his wits
and out of anger started cursing loudly.
Then as his anger waned he thought it better
to join the gods and try resolve the matter.

Si vidinu arrivari, in atti illiciti.
Stizzatu ognunu e ccu lu cazzu tisu;
Chi cc'è ? cci dici: vi faciti liciti
Fari sti cosi, senza darmi avvisu ?
Cchiù non si pigghia a mia lu benediciti,
Menzi culiddi di lu paradisu?
Chi sù davanti a mia sti cazzi in autu ?
Chi vi mancia la garra, o siti in sautu ?

Iu ccu vuatri non vogghiu cummattiri,
Si no vi mannu a farivi strafuttiri.
L'alma, dissi la Dia, mi sentu abattiri,
Papà, non aju ciatu, 'un pozzu agghiuttiri
Ch'era locca oimè d'occhi fra un battiri,
Ognunu mi dicia lassiti futtiri:
Sta cosa non cumprennu in virità;
Futtiri, chi significa, Papà?

Ah! becchi strafuttuti, vastasuna,
Grida arraggiatu comu tigri ircana,
Cussì si tratta ccu la mia pirsuna,
Veri garrusi e figghi di buttana ?
La pigghiastivu forsi, o gran minchiuna,
Pri la Baciccia, o pri la Girgintana?
Vi pari cosa di Numi perfetti
Scannaliari li picciotti schetti ?

Pocu cci staiu cca pri mia vinditta
A cauci e timpuluni 'un vi nni mannu;
Comu li denti di nna vecchia affritta
Chiddi allura ammutiscinu, trimannu.
Sulu li minchi ristaru a l'addritta,
Nè l'arrittu cci passa finu a tannu:
Pirchì si dici: ca cazzu arrittatu
Non canusci rispettu e parintatu.

The gods who were caught in illicit acts,
and with dicks hard were miffed and quite upset
"What's this," he said to them, "You have the gall
to do these things without a word to me?
You do not need permission any more,
little half-asses out of paradise?
How daré you show yourselves with such hard cocks?
What's itching you? Your brains are filled with rocks?

I've no desire to start thrashing you
or I would really kick your butts to hell."
"Daddy," the goddess said. "My heart is beating,
I'm out of breath, I cannot even swallow.
With one more thrust I would have lost my mind,
They kept repeating, *let me fuck you, please!*
I just don't understand the words they said!
What is the meaning of this *fucking*, Dad?"

"You sorry and ill-mannered awful boors!"
Jove started yelling like a Persian tiger.
"Is this the way you treat my holy being,
you veritable fags, sons of a bitch?
Did you mistake her for a whore, you fools,
like the Baciccia or the Girgintana?
You think it's seemly for a perfect god
to show a virgin his tumescent rod?"

"I do not know why I am holding back,
why I don't kick your butts to kingdom come."
The gods fell silent and began to shake,
like an old lady's teeth who's seen a ghost.
Only their dicks remained straight and erect.
Nor did their hard-on give signs of abating,
for it's well known, *a dick that is erect
acknowledges no kin nor shows respect.*

Parentisi: quantunchi a tempi tali
Baciccia e Girgintana 'un si numava;
Puru lu summu Giovi, Diu immurtali.
Già lu capiti, ca prufitizzava;
Li figghi soi non eranu minnali;
La prufizia perciò Giovi parrava
Di buttani futuri 'ntra dd'istanti
Comu di lu prisenti e stipulanti.

Sta facenna però, Giovi ripigghia,
S'avi aggiustari, giacchì sta canagghia
M'avi scannaliata sta mia figghia
Pura, comu nasciu di la 'nfasciagghia;
'Npulisativi, ed una si nni pigghia,
E cui 'ntra l'unghia di la sorti 'ngagghia,
E nesci 'ntra vuiatri bonavogghia,
Cci la ficca à rumpiricci la mogghia.

Dici: e li nomi a Ganimedi additta,
E a lu latu di Veniri s'assetta;
Stannu li cincu Dii tutti all'addritta,
Comu lu reu chi la sintenza aspetta:
Giovi stissu si leva la birritta,
E dda dintra li polisi cci jetta;
Veniri afferra 'na polisa in manu,
E si leggi lu nomu di Vulcanu.

"Nota: non avi a fari maravigghia
Di un matrimoniu d'un frati e 'nna soru;
Pirchì quannu non c'era gran famigghia,
Sti matrimoni prima accussì foru:
La futtuta di Lot ccu la figghia
Fu di la Chiesa cilibrata a coru.
Iu dunca, opera strana non la chiamu
La futtuta surastra; sicutamu!"

Parenthesis: Although Baciccia's name
and Girgintana's were not known back then,
you readily can see that mighty Jove,
immortal god, the future was foretelling.
His children were not stupid nincompoops,
so Jove in prophesying simply spoke
of these two present whores who staked their claims
to future being as he gave them names.

"This matter clearly must be set to right,"
Jove said continuing. "These awful boors
have so defiled my innocent young child
who was as pure as when she was in diapers.
Let's choose a lot and she will have the one
who happens to get caught beneath Fate's nail,
and he who's winner of the final bout
has my permission to screw her brains out."

He spoke and gave the names to Ganymede.
Then he proceeded to sit next to Venus.
The five divinities stood at attention,
like poor defendants waiting to be sentenced.
Then Jove himself took off the hat he wore
and threw the markers with the names in it.
Venus reached in to start the picking game
and then proceeded to read Vulcan's name.

A note: it should be no surprise to you
to learn about the wedding of two siblings,
'cause when the human family was small,
a brother and his sister could unite.
So when Lot fornicated with his daughter
the Church in chorus celebrated it.
Therefore, I do not deem it a strange deed
to fuck your sister: so let us proceed!"

87

Non curri, si pricipita, anzi vola
Vulcanu ch'avi la gamma sciancata:
L'abbrazza, e vola, e perdi la parola
Dda picciotta stringennusi sciacquata.
Giovi cci dici: figghia, ti cunsola,
Ti binidicu la prima minchiata.
Vulcanu intantu senz'autra licenza
La metti a terra, sbrogghia, ed accumenza.

Prima l'afferra ccu duci carizzi
L'affumicata celibri minchiazza:
Idda si fa la facci pizzi pizzi,
Iddu cci metti 'mpocu di sputazza,
Ma ora l'ura chi vennu li sbrizzi,
Iddu stenni nna manu a la spaccazza
E tastiannu la pilusa rocca
Cerca, afferra, mania, tocca e ritocca,

Tuccannu e rituccannu cunnu e culu,
Non ha paci si tutta 'un ci la metti:
Cci va supra arrittatu comu un mulu,
E cci stringi li minni, e la scunnetti.
Di dui corpi si fici un corpu sulu
Li vrazza si cuntorcinu a li petti,
E uniti comu stannu corda e sicchiu,
Panza e panza si adatta, e cazzu e sticchiu.

'Mpugna ddu sulennissimu rapista,
E 'ntra nna fedda e l'autra l'assesta;
Ietta un gran corpu arrabbiatu in vista,
Ma cci 'ngagghiau la minchia menza testa.
Nisciuta un pocu, nova forza acquista
La 'mpugna arreri, ci la metti, arresta;
Poi dintra imputusa ci la scagghia,
Ma'ntra lu megghiu di lu corpu ammagghia.

Vulcan didn't run, he hurtled, nay, he flew
despite the fact that he had one lame leg.
He clasped that wondrous beauty to his chest,
with much excitement, nearly out of breath.
Jove said to her: "My daughter be content!
Your very first fuck I hereby do bless."
Then Vulcan without wasting any time,
placed her upon the ground, undressed and climbed.

He started by caressing her sweet face and head,
then he applied his famous smoke-stained dick.
Her face, however, started to turn red.
So he put some saliva on his prick.
This was no time to stop: full steam ahead!
He reached with his large hand into her crack
and feeling all about the hairy mound,
he touched and squeezed, he grabbed and poked around.

Upon her ass and pussy he just drooled.
He would not rest until he'd plugged that hole.
He mounted her as though he'd been a mule,
grabbing her teats and jostling that poor soul.
One body was then blended from two breasts,
their frenzied arms were twined around their chests
and they were tightly bound as flame to wick,
belly to belly, pussy facing dick.

That celebrated lover grabbed his cock
and placed it in the center of her crack,
then he unleashed a mighty forward thrust,
but managed to wedge in part of his prick.
After withdrawing to pick up more strength,
he grabbed his dick, he placed it and he paused.
Then with a mighty thrust he pushed it in,
but it got stuck halfway inside her yin.

Era nica la porta e non trasia,
Ca nuddu ancora cci l'avia ficcatu:
Veniri a lu duluri si turcia,
Già si abbannuna e non avi chiù ciatu;
Qualchi stizza di sangu si vidia
Dintra ddu sticchiareddu dilicatu:
Chiddi carni parianu virmigghi,
Comu la paparina 'ntra li gigghi.

Trasi... nesci... fa... leva... ficca... basti
Forti... adaciu... dicia... fermiti... ammutta.
Ahi chi corpu! ahi chi chiaja! ahi m'ammazzasti!
Nescila!... non ti moviri... cchiù sutta.
Quali balsamu scurri! chi mi dasti?
Trasi cchiù dintra, ficcamilla tutta:
Lassala stari, via, comu fu fu;
Chi è duci! Chi piaciri! 'un pozzu cchiù!

Eccu frattantu un lavizzu di spacchiu
Ca scurri comu scurri un canalicchiu:
Comu abbucca rumpennusi 'mpinnacchiu,
Veniri allasca lu so beddu sicchiu.
Vulcanu cci lassau lu grossu cacchiu
Pri menz'ura 'nfilatu 'ntra lu sticchiu.
E intantu a maniari si trattinni
Facci, pettu, masciddi, culu e minni.

A ddi modi, a ddi gesti a chiddi atti,
Ristanu l'autri ammaluccuti e afflitti,
Friddi comu la nivi e stupefatti,
Comu pasturi ca gran lupu vitti.
Giovi cci dici: cci sù mezzi adatti
Pri a vuatri passarivi l'arritti:
La minata iu criai pri cui non futti.
Basta ca v'aiu cunsulatu a tutti.

The gate just would not budge, as it was smallish,
because no man had ever entered it.
Venus was reeling from the pain and anguish.
She gasped for air and nearly lost her wits,
as drops of blood began to trickle out
from that most delicate sweet pussy's mouth.
Her flesh was stained with a vermilion blight,
resembling poppies in a field of white.

In... out...some heavy thrusts...withdraws again...
"Enough! Easy now...Push hard... please stop!
Not so hard... oh the pain...you're killing me!
Please, take it out! No, do not move, lay down!
What balm is flowing now? What did you give me?
A little more! Oh, shove it deeper into me!
Stay like that, let it be, no matter what!
Oh pleasure, there is no sweetness quite like that!"

But in the meantime, like a flowing stream,
his come had started gushing into her.
As when a pole is broken and hangs limp,
so Venus let her tunnel grow relaxed.
Vulcan just let his heavy cock remain
engorged inside her hole for half an hour.
Meanwhile to pass the time he stroked one breast,
fondling her face, her jaws, her ass and chest.

On seeing all their gestures and their deeds,
the other gods were stunned and in despair,
frozen like blocks of ice and without breath,
like shepherds who have seen a pack of wolves.
Jove said to them: I have devised a way
to make all your erections disappear.
Now masturbation I create for you:
it is my gift to those who do not screw.

Dissi: ed ognunu la pistola 'griddu
La nesci, e si la metti a lu scupertu,
Russa la testa comu lu cardiddu,
L'occhi alli minni ed a lu culu apertu;
Unu l'afferra a nautru, e chistu a chiddu;
Tra d'iddi si la minanu a cuncertu;
E situannu li manuzzi a granciu
Si la jocanu tutti a canciu e scanciu.

Cci mettunu sputazza a gran vuccuna,
E applicannucci poi l'intinzioni,
Si dannu corpa alla diavulina.
Senza tanticchia di discrizioni.
Eccu lu semi ca nesci a frusciuna,
Cci riscaldau l'immaginazioni;
Ristaru comu tanti varvajanni,
Ccu n'occhiu a Cristu e nautru a S. Ciuvanni.*

*Cu l'occhi stralunati

92

After he spoke each of the gods took out
his pistol and he openly displayed it:
the heads were red like those of cardinals.
While staring at her teats and at her ass,
each held his dick or grabbed somebody else's.
They started masturbating one another.
Moving their hands in backward crablike motion,
they stroked each other, making a commotion.

They then applied saliva by the mouthfuls
and with sheer dedication and resolve,
without the least discretion or regard,
they beat their meat like devils on a rampage,
The semen started flowing like a flood
which heated their imagination even more.
At last, they all remained dismayed and wan,
one eye to Christ, the other to St. John.*

*Looking dazed and cross-eyed.

La Monica Dispirata

Sula sula 'ntra stu lettu
Li nuttati aju a passari:
Nuddu giuvini a stu pettu
A mia tocca d'abbrazzari.

Sticchiu miu rispittuseddu,
Senza minchia ca ti strigghia!
E sulu c'un ghiditeddu
Ca li labbra ti cattigghia;

Pri tia certu cci vurria
Un battagghiu di campana,
Ca la forma pigghiria
Di nna grossa minchia umana.

Si pulitu e graziusu,
Nudda lingua mai t'allicca;
Nuddu cazzu impituusu
Dintra a tia mai si cc'inficca.

Quanti fimmini a stu munnu
Cci sù stati, e cci sarannu
Ca minchiati 'ntra lu cunnu
Nn'anu avutu e n'avirannu!

Ed iu sula ventu abbrazzu;
Si mi votu e mi stinnicchiu
Mai non trovu nuddu cazzu
Pri ficcallu 'ntra stu sticchiu:

Cci nni sunnu 'ntra quarteri
Grossi minchi di surdati,
Ca 'ntra d'iddi lu darreri,
Si lu pigghiunu arraggiati.

The Desperate Nun

Quite forlorn in this poor bed
I must spend the nights alone.
Oh my destiny is sad,
with no young man of my own!

Oh dear pussy, so discreet,
I've no cock to spread my hips.
I have just a little finger
that can tickle your sweet lips.

You deserved, for heaven's sake,
the large knocker of a bell
that a human form would take
like the big cock of a man.

You're a clean and pretty sight,
but no tongue has licked you yet,
not one cock have you yet met,
who has shown you all its might.

Countless women in the world,
in the present and the past,
whose sweet pussies have been fucked
and will be till time will last!

I alone embrace the air!
If I turn and stretch to see
not a cock can I find there
I can shove inside of me.

There are soldiers' brawny cocks,
who are quartered in our town,
who assault each other's asses
with a mean and angry frown.

'Ntra cunventi cci nni sunnu
Beddi minchi rancitusi,
Non avennu nuddu cunnu,
Si li minanu oziusi:

'Ntra campagni rocchi e margi
Cci sù certi viddanuni,
Ch'annu minchi ccu li jargi
Peju assai di li stadduni.

E tu, sticchiu, li disii,
Comu l'erva a marzu pioggia,
Svinturatu lacrimii,
Non c'è cazzu ca t'alloggia.

Minchia mia di stu miu cori,
'Nzuccarata minchia mia!
Stu me cori spinna e mori,
Suffrirà senza di tia.

Fusti fatta 'ntra lu munnu
Di la provvida Natura,
Pri ficcarti 'ntra lu cunnu
D'ogni nata criatura.

Quali fimmina pò stari
Senza sticchiu arriminatu?
Non è nenti lu mangiari,
Pri cui futtiri ha gustatu.

Quannu poi futtiri s'avi,
Pri precettu di Natura,
Lu 'mpararu li nannavi.
Si nni parra doppu un'ura.

Ma a chi servi stu riflessi
Si lu cunnu sta in ruina ?
Megghiu è assai l'umanu sessu
Chi a lu ventu si la mina:

In the monasteries, too,
languish handsome cocks galore.
And since pussies monks can't screw,
they jerk off forever more.

In the country there are hicks
whose strong backs are straight as rods,
who have formidable dicks
even bigger than a stud's.

And you, pussy, yearn in vain,
as in March grass yearns for rain;
wretched pussy, you just cry:
you've no cock with which to play.

Oh sweet cock, dear to my heart,
sugar coated dick of mine!
How my suffering does smart!
I will die, too much I pine.

You were made for just one duty
by the providence of Nature:
to find shelter in the booty
of the females of our creatures.

Say, what woman can relax
if her pussy you don't stir?
For once you have tasted sex,
there's no food that can compare.

Once you've chosen to start screwing,
follow old folks and our nature
who taught that if it's worth doing,
you must do it at your leisure.

But why ponder such a matter,
with my pussy, oh so bare?
The male organ is much better:
you can beat it in the air!

E ci senti lu piaciri
Quannu è l'ura di jittari
Ma nna donna avi a muriri
Ca non avi chi minari.

Oh! si avissi pri menz'ura
Ccu mia un giuvini curcatu.
Ccu na minchia grossa e dura
Chi futtissi arrabbiatu,

Futti, futti, cci dirria:
Tè ccà, afferriti a sti minni;
Sta pirsuna è data a tia;
Tò stu sticchiu: saziatinni!

Tè sta lingua; suchimmilla,
Muncimillu stu capicchiu;
Sta pirsuna pir tia brilla;
Sugnu to e to stu sticchiu.

Chi sì duci! chi sì beddu!
Vurria nautru gustu sulu;
Ficchimillu un ghiditeddu,
Ca mi piaci 'ntra lu culu!

Comu vonnu li prammatichi
Pri lu cazzu non sgriddari,
Ccu la panza, ccu li natichi,
Iu mi mettu a cazziari.

Ma chi fazzu ? ccu cui futtu?
Ccu la sula fantasia ?
Ah! non viu quantu è bruttu
Senza minchia cca nni mia!

Iu pri un cazzu canciria
Li tisori di lu munnu;
E macari cci darria
Li pilidda di stu cunnu.

You can feel then the great pleasure
when your climax is complete.
But a woman has no treasure:
no sweet meat that she can beat!

Oh if only for half hour
I could have right next to me
a young dick that's full of power
that would fuck me hungrily.

Fuck me, fuck me, I would say:
my whole body's yours to take,
take my teats, hang on and sway!
Here's my pussy, do partake!

Suck my tongue, see how it yearns!
Squeeze my nipples till they hurt!
My whole body aches and burns.
I am yours, my pussy yours.

How delicious, a sweet nut!
Satisfy another whim!
Stick a finger up my butt,
for I like it so like that!

As prescribed by etiquette,
to hold off a cock's last sigh
I'll just rub my belly on it,
and I'll stroke it with my thighs.

What a fool! Who am I screwing?
Is it just a fantasy?
How depressing all this cooing
with no dick here next to me!

I'd give up all treasures quick
just to have here a hard dick.
I would pluck my pubic hair
and my pussy leave all bare!

Si mi votu supra e sutta
E lu pilu 'ncrispa e rizza,
Scafuniu, mi futtu tutta;
Non c'è gustu senza pizza!

'Ntra stu puntu futtiria
Ccu curaggiu chiù trimennu;
E si poi nni muriria,
Muriria sempri futtennu!

Nici (1)

Caddu! Nici, tu sì gravida !
Ah, cui fu chiss'assurtatu,
Chi ficcau un cazzu pantoticu
'Ntra ssu sticchiu almu e beatu?

Iu la sorti non invidiu
Di ssu cazzu, amata Nici;
Sulu ciangiu, ch'iu ccu l'autri
Non potti essiri felici.

Comu! dunca mentri in lagrimi
Si struggia stu cori invanu,
Tu tinevi pr'arraspariti
Lu stadduni suttamanu!

E ssu sticchiu mai placabili
Nè a prieri nè a ragiuni,
Minchi, comu gloria patiri,
S'agghiutteva all'ammucciuni?

Pri spiegari stu misteriu
Non ho ciatu, nè palori
Cazzu! è cosa impercettibili
D'una fimmina lu cori!

I turn left, then I turn right,
my hair's twisted in a tangle.
I am screwed from every angle:
but the pizza's just not right!

At this juncture I would fuck
mighty boldly, without dread;
if while screwing I dropped dead,
I'd consider it my luck.

Nice (1)

Damn it! Nice, you are pregnant!
Say who was the lucky soul
who stuck in his mighty pendant
in your sweet and blessed hole?

It 's not that I can't digest
that dick's fortune who screwed you;
I regret with all the rest
that my wish could not come true.

So while this poor heart of mine
was despairing - what a bitch!-
you a stallion had on line
who would scratch your every itch?

And your misanthropic pussy
which no prayer could convince,
was in gulping dicks so busy
you'd have thought them wafer thins?

Say what words, what human art,
can explain this mystery?
Damn it! How a woman's heart
functions most inscrutably!

Tutti, oddiu! bugiardi e perfidi.
Tutti siti d'una pasta:
Comu ! Nici si fa futtiri.
E pareva la chiù casta!

A Nici (V)

Nici, mi vinni un nolitu
Di futtiri all'inglisa;
ca sugnu arrittatissimu:
talè chi minchia tisa!

Lu gustu è inesplicabili,
si tasti 'un ti lu scordi:
Di sta manera futtinu
Li nobili milordi.

Annunca, prestu curcati,
lu lettu è già cunzatu,
non haiu chiù pacenzia
pri mia sugnu spugghiatu

La sorti n'è propizia
futtemu allegramenti;
non servi accussì perdiri
st'amabili mumenti.

Mettiti a panza all'aria,
chista è la moda Ircana,
li bianchi cosci gnuttica
a modu di giurana.

Assumma, Nici amabili,
iu futtu e tu cazzii;
fammi satari all'aria
finu ca ti nichii.

You're all hateful, lying, shrews!
You're all made from the same paste.
Fathom this! My Nice screws
and she seemed so pure, so chaste!

To Nice (V)

I got a notion, Nice,
to fuck you English style;
look how my eager Chee-chee
stands all ready and virile!

I can't explain the pleasure.
You won't forget its taste!
This is a British treasure,
that's how the Lords all screw.

So quickly come to bed,
for it's already made.
You see, my clothes I've shed.
I'm eager to get laid.

Luck here is on our side.
Let's screw with joy and cheer!
Let's move along in stride.
Don't waste a moment, Dear!

Lie on your back, I pray,
this is the Turkish way
and bend your thigh and leg
as though you were a frog.

So Nice raise your thigh
and take in my whole loaf,
and make me jump quite high
until you've had enough.

Chi centru matematicu,
chi calculu profunnu!
Vih comu si cummattinu
la cazzu cu lu cunnu!

A lu cudduzzu accucciati
e iu a li to spadduzzi,
a li me gammi afferrrati
e iu a li to cosciuzzi.

Li minni e li to natichi
sunna na vera scuma,
mi parinu dui provuli
chiù bianchi di la tuma.

Va... prestu Nici, vasami,
nesci la to linguzza,
cu la me lingua nsemula
facemu na sirpuzza.

Vidi c'abbassa l'utiru
sinu l'immuccatura?
Disidira sucarisi
l'umana rinnitura.

Cazzu, chi beddu futtiri,
Chi gustu prilibatu !
Chistu è lu veru futtiri:
L'inglisi sia ludatu!

What perfect math this is,
what wondrous calculation!
Behold how dicks and pussies
can manage copulation!

Hold on to my strong neck
and to your shoulder I,
my legs now keep in check
while I rein in your thigh.

What buttocks and what teats!
They're truly like sea foam,
they are for me such treats,
much sweeter than whipped cream.

Come give me a sweet kiss.
Nice, give me your tongue.
Let's snake our way to bliss
entwining both of them.

Your uterus is low
down to the entrance hole,
the better to cajole
the human liquid flow.

To screw like this is grand!
What an exquisite taste,
the best in all the land!
The English lords be praised!

Lu diliriu

Si t'aggranciu, amatu Numi,
'Ntra sti corri, amara tia!
Di ss'amabili lattumi
Chi macellu nni faria!

D'ogni puntu, d'ogni latu
Perliccannu a stizza a stizza,
Mi vidrissi un affamatu
Divorarmi ssa biddizza.

Chi sebbeni è tanta e tali
Ch'è infinita e mai non speddi,
Faria cuntu e capitali
Di li stissi muddicheddi.

Cussì sulu putria un pocu
Sudisfari li mei brami,
Astutari stu gran focu,
Saturarmi di sta fami.

'Ntra ssi morbidi e ciuriti,
Vaghi e turgidi giardini,
O chi frutti assai squisiti
iu cugghissi a manu chini!

Mentri in senu a sti diletti
Sugnu assortu, o vita mia,
Tra un dilluviu d'affetti
Quantu cosi ti dirria!

Chi momentu fortunatu
In vidirmi a tia vicinu!
Ma in miu dannu s'è ostinatu
L'implacabili distinu.

Love Madness

If I get you in my claws,
my dear goddess, woe is you!
What destruction I would cause
on your tender milk white flesh!

As a man who's starved to death
from all sides at every hour
I would linger on your breath
your sweet beauty to devour,

and although it is so vast
that it's boundless, without end,
I would still not care to waste
the most tiny bit of you.

Only thus could I aspire
to fulfill all my desire,
to throw water on this fire,
and my hunger pacify.

In your soft and flowered garden,
so splendiferous and grand
o what ripe, exquisite fruits
I would harvest with both hands!

And as I am all absorbed
in the midst of such delights,
in a deluge of emotions
What sweet things would I recite!

Oh how lucky I would be
to be near to you this way!
But my heartless destiny
to my ruin has conspired.

Passu, ohimè! jurnati interi
'Ntra stu miu vaneggiamentu;
Sù delirii, e sù pinseri
Ca si perdunu a lu ventu.

Duci amuri, amatu beni,
Nudda cosa mi cunforta.
Sunnu eterni li mei peni.
La spiranza è quasi morta.

'Ntra st'amuri, e quali arcanu
Si nascondi, o miu tesoru!
Chi mi arrassa, e fa luntanu
Stu disiu, pri cui nni moru!

Sarà forsi, chi lu fatu,
Scatinannu soi fururi,
Pri pietà d'un svinturatu,
Usa a mia tantu riguri.

Chi si un giornu cancia aspettu
Lu distinu, e sarai mia,
Pr'un eccessu di dilettu
La mia vita finiria.

Lu sceccu e lu liuni

Sempri haju 'ntisu diri pr'accussì,
Una risposta data a tempu e a locu
Quannu cci voli accattala un tarì.

Però, ma in suli termini di jocu
Chistu è permissu, e non in serii affari
Ca la morali si risenti un pocu.

Pirchì duvemu tuttu suppurtari
Ccu pazienza e bona vuluntati,
Pirchì è malignità lu vindicari.

I now spend, alas, whole days
lost in such vain fantasies:
It is madness: thoughts that sway
in the wind and then are gone.

My sweet love, beloved love
I see everything with dread.
Everlasting are my woes
and my hope is nearly dead.

What a mystery holds sway
in this loving, my sweet treasure,
that can keep me far away
from my wish and make me die?

Could it be that destiny
which unleashed on me such slaughter,
has let loose its fury so
in compassion for another?

But if destiny one day
should relent and you were mine,
through an excess of sheer joy
my life would come to an end.

The Donkey and the Lion

I've heard that when you must give a riposte,
appropriately, at the right time and place,
you should not worry much about its cost.

However, this is valid in the case
we're playing games, not when the thrust
is serious. Then morals you'd debase.

That's so because without complaint we must
endure all things with patience and good will.
To seek revenge is evil and unjust.

Ma lu sceccu fratantu in serietati
Prujiu la so risposta, ed iu vi dicu
Ca cci vinni di vera asinitati.

Pirchì lu sceccu ha pri custumi anticu
D'essiri bestia, zoticu e 'ngnuranti,
Malucriatu e d'onestà nemicu.

Non ha religioni e mancu santi,
E' tistarutu, e com'iddu la senti
Accussì la discurri, e passa avanti.

Eranu un ghiornu, o fu per accidenti,
O pri soi proprii affari, a un gran viaggiu
L'asinu e lu liuni assemi intenti.

Parravanu pri strata in sò linguaggiu
Lu liuni di stragi e di rapina,
Lu sceccu di furraina e d'erbaggiu.

Fratantu discurrennu su vicini
A un ciumi, a cui lu liquefattu jazzu
Li matarazzi a tippu cci avia chini.

Lu sceccu ch'era un veru flosofazzu
Dissi: sti ciumi pri cui si ritrova
In viaggiu, sempri portanu 'mbarazzu.

L'acqua è un fluidu chi vagna, e sacciu a prova
C'arrimodda ogni cosa, e testimoniu
Nni sia lu baccalaru robba nova.

Perciò ccu l'armi di lu matrimoniu
In vidirla nui scecchi ad anchi aperti
Cci pisciamu la sditta e lu dimoniu.

E già si sapi, e non si controverti
(Rispunniu lu liuni a so cumpari)
Ca sempri siti stati genti sperti.

Although the donkey gave his answer, still,
it proved his utter asininity,
in spite the fact he showed a certain skill.

By ancient custom donkeys seem to be
uncouth and stubborn and know-nothing beasts,
dumb and ill-mannered foes of honesty.

With no religion, they observe no feast.
They act exactly how they feel inside.
For others' thoughts they are concerned the least.

A donkey and a lion, brought side by side,
either by accident or common goals,
were traveling together quite in stride.

They talked along their journey in their roles.
The lion spoke of slaughtering and schemes,
the donkey dwelled on grass and oats in bowls.

As they were talking, they approached a stream
whose bed the mountain's melting snows had filled
so high it threatened to burst at the seam.

The donkey, a wise beast, this sentence spilled:
"Such rivers one encounters on the way
are truly bothersome, say what you will!

Speaking from true experience, I say
that water is a fluid that is wet
which soaks through, think of cod that once was dry.

So when we donkeys see a rivulet,
we spread our legs and with the arm we use
to wed we pee to show we are upset."

"And everybody knows how truly wise
a race of animals you donkeys are!"
the king of beasts then noddingly replies.

Perciò duvennu tutti dui passari
Stu ciumi, è conseguenza indubitata
Ca nni duvemu tutti dui vagnari.

La cosa è troppu beni dimustrata
Pri duvirni vagnari tutti dui,
Ma sintiti com'iu l'haju pinsata.

Iu per esemplu m'accavarcu a vui,
E vui purtati a mia, eccuti iu sentu
Ca si vagna unu sulu, e nuddu chiui.

Ma sidd'iu vi ritorciu l'argumentu,
Arrispusi lu sceccu, iu senza stenti
Vi 'nsaccu ccu lu vostru sentimentu.

E ragiuni non cc'è sufficienti
Fra mia e vui, e non mi rispunniti
Ca vui siti liuni ed iu su nenti.

Ripigghia lu liuni: 'un vogghiu liti,
Semu cumpari, avemu a stari in paci,
Non siati sufisticu, e sintiti:

Iu d'ingannarvi non sarò capaci;
Pr'ora purtati a mia, poi a la turnata
Iu portu a vui, non sacciu si vi piaci.

Lu sceccu aveva un obicies, e data,
Dissi, sta liggi tra di nui, non pozzu
Forsi aviri da vui nna birbantata?

Chistu sarrà un pinsari assai spopozzu
Di l'azioni mei, l'autru rispunni,
E cci accavarca e s'afferra a lu cozzu.

S'incammina lu sceccu in menzu all'unni,
E comu va trasennu, accussì crisci
La ciumara, e su l'acqui chiù profunni.

"It's clear we have to cross this stream, therefore,
it is incontrovertible that we,
in fording will get soaked through every pore.

There are no ways around this, as you see.
We'll soak our bones completely through and through.
But I've devised a plan. If you agree,

I could, for instance, climb on top of you,
and you will carry me across the stream.
This way one only will get wet, not two!"

The donkey thoughtfully replied: "Your scheme
can easily be worked the other way.
Why should I be the first one in this team?

No reason why I should do what you say.
- Please spare me the predictable reply
that you're the lion and that I'm the prey!"

The lion answered him: "Let us both try
to get along. I do not want to fight;
We are good friends. Don't try to mystify!

I won't be able to deceive you, friend!
This time you'll carry me, when we return
you'll ride on me, instead. You comprehend?"

The donkey then inquired cautiously:
"Given this pact between us, can you swear
that you will not behave most scoundrelly?"

"Your judgment of my actions is unfair,
unjust!" the other animal replied,
making himself the donkey's new neckwear.

But as the ass began to wade inside
the stream, the level of the water rose,
making him sink much deeper in the tide.

Già si vagna li naschi, e cci finisci
La terra da li pedi, e a branchi stisi
Sbruffa 'ntra l'unni, e nata comu un pisci.

L'intrepidu liuni ben cumprisi
Lu periculu unn'era, e l'ugna azzicca,
S'aggrancia forti, e si teni a li prisi.

E tantu 'ntra la peddi cci li ficca
Ca lu sceccu cu tuttu ddu 'mbarazzu
Trasiri si li 'ntisi, e non fu picca.

E barbuttannu 'ntra l'undusu sguazzu,
Cumpari, ci dicia, non su azioni,
Di farini di mia tantu strapazzu.

Lu liuni pri livarlu d'apprensioni
Rispunniu: l'ugna mei sù un pocu storti:
E mi non cascu iu l'appizzu boni;

Si tratta di periculu di morti:
Si m'anneiu è finuta, amicu caru,
Perciò bisogna chiù mi tegnu forti.

Dunca faciti vui, dissi l'amaru,
Ca poi fazz'iu. Fratantu a sarvamentu
Sunnu arrivati 'ntra l'oppostu scaru.

E passatu lu scantu e lu spaventu,
Si misiru in caminu, e accumpagnati
Purtaru li soi affari a cumpimentu.

Ecculi di belnovu riturnati
Sunnu a lu stissu ciumi. Nellu casu
Di passarlu com'eranu appuntati.

Lu sceccu ch'un si passa musca a nasu,
Si ferma e dici: già lu pattu è fattu;
Cridu chi ristiriti persuasu;

The level with the water reached his nose.
He started splashing, swimming like a fish,
struggling against the wave and undertows.

The danger that he faced passed in a flash
before the daring lion's eyes who dug
his claws much deeper to avoid the splash

into the waves. But from the lion's hug
the wretched donkey felt some awful pain.
—You can't dismiss those sharp nails with a shrug!—

And as he swam he started to complain:
"My friend," he mumbled, "You are killing me!
You have no right to cause me so much pain!"

The lion reassured the animal:
"My claws are bent a bit, I know it well.
I'm simply holding on so I won't fall.

But I am risking death, as you can tell.
If I should drown, it's over, my good friend!
That's why I dig my claws. What if I fell?"

"Do what you must, for later I intend
to do my part," the hapless donkey said,
as they crossed safely to the other end.

When fear and dread had started to abate,
they went on with their journey earnestly
and once their dealings were complete,

they came back to the place where they had crossed
and paused a while where they had stood before.
With roles reversed, they had to go across.

The donkey is a beast that keeps good score.
He stopped and said: "The pact we made is clear!
I don't believe that we can say much more."

E pinsiriti quali fu lu pattu
Conclusu tra di nui, e quantu, e comu
Sia la palora chiù di lu contrattu.

Ma lu liuni ch'era un galantomu,
Rispusi: 'n cc'è facciazza, iu sù custanti
E chi niscissi a mia l'ultimu sbromu.

Isa lu sceccu li pedi d'avanti,
E cci accavarca ccu tanta modestia
Ca pari un fratacchiuni zucculanti.

Cussì accavaddu l'una all'autra bestia
Vannu, e lu sceccu (pri cui tuttu è licitu)
Una cosa pinsava assai smodesta.

E misu pr'accussì sbrogghia sullicitu
Lu quintu pedi, risolutu a fari
Lu chiù nefandu matrimoniu illicitu.

Comu 'nfatti principia a tastiari,
Fissa lu puntu ccu dda so olivastra
Armatura terribili a guardari.

E poi di schinu ccu nna botta mastra
Cc'immergi in senu (Diu nni pò scanzari)
Longa quant'è dd'orrenda palacastra.

Lu liuni si 'ntisi appiccicari
Un focu a lu pretteritu perfettu,
E ghietta un gridu ca lu fa spirdari.

E' chista nna mancanza di rispettu.
Lu diavulu in corpu mi trasiu,
Livatimillu dunca ccà vi jettu.

Lu sceccu cu nna flemma di Judiu,
Pacenzia, cci dissi: chi vuliti ?
Non haju autru. Chistu è l'ugnu miu.

"You know exactly what you said down here,
and how we both agreed. Now keep your word.
A word's more than a contract, if sincere."

The lion was an honest beast and heard
the ass: "I'm not two-faced, I'm constant, straight.
If I renege, may I become a turd!"

The ass raised his front legs, put all his weight
on his hind legs and climbed upon the king
with such demureness he seemed a prelate.

The donkey, riding on the beastly king,
was planning — donkeys know no boundaries —
to implement a most indecent thing.

As soon as he was seated in his place,
the ass unfurled his fifth leg and prepared
a most illicit union to emplace.

So he began to probe as to locate
the spot and placed the tip of his dark-skinned
awesome and fear inspiring heavyweight,

then with a master stroke at first he pinned
the lion, then he drove his member's length
into the unsuspecting and chagrined

king of the beasts, who felt its awesome strength.
His poor derriere was burning from the pain.
He screamed so loudly that his might was spent.

"This is an awful breach, a shameful sin!
You stuck the very devil in my ass!
Remove it quickly or I'll throw you in!"

With the aloofness of a Jew, the ass
replied, "Have patience. What am I to do?
This is my only claw! I've nothing else.

Lu periculu è granni, lu sapiti,
Ed iu non haju pri mia mala sorti
Autru puntu d'appoggiu; lu viditi.

L'ugna mei non sù dritti, nè sù storti,
Ma sulu stu strumentu di lussuria,
Quannu vaju accavaddu mi fa forti;

Cumpari miu, risposta non è ingiuria.

La prima sira

—Ora ca semu suli
ni divirtemu, o Nici,
truvari non putemu
mumenti chiù filici.

M'arrozzulu a spugghiari
li robbi, sauta jettu,
eccu ca sugnu lestu,
mi ficcu nta lu lettu.

Ma tu non m'arrispunni,
mi fai l'addurmisciuta;
risbigghiati, curuzzu,
facemu na futtuta.

—Ivih! chi granni chiacchira
vi vinni sta nuttata!
Durmemu, cuitativi,
già m'ava appinnicata.

—Di dormiri tu parri?
Stasira? La sgarrasti.
Chi dormiri... chi dici?
Finemu sti cuntrasti.

The dangers we are facing are not few!
And I, to my misfortune, have no claws
to steady me, except the rod I put in you!

My nails are not so crooked nor so long.
This instrument of lust is my defense.
When I'm on top, this is what makes me strong.

Friend, giving tit for tat is no offense!"

The First Night

"Now that we are alone
we'll have a ball, my Nice.
A more propitious time
we cannot hope to find.

You see how I am rushing
to put away my clothes;
I'm rushing to get ready
and jump into our bed.

But you don't answer me,
pretending you're asleep.
Awaken, my sweet wife,
and let's make love at last."

"What's gotten into you?
You're talkative tonight.
I was almost asleep,
I'd started to doze off."

"You talk of dozing off?
This night? You got it wrong.
What sleep, what are you saying?
Let's stop this bickering.

Lassa ca ccu sti manu
li minni t'affirrassi
e li capicchi amabili
la vucca mia sucassi.

—Figghioli, chi brivogna!
M'affruntu, in viritati,
calativi sti manu,
lu pettu non tuccati...

—Tuccannu sti minnuzzi,
sta minchia mia s'arritta.
Dammi la manu, o Nici,
vidi com'è a l'additta?

—Ivih! Chi cosa longa!
Chi è sta cosa tisa?
—Vòtati a gammi all'aria,
isati la cammisa.

Chissa na lu to schicchiu
ti l'haiu iu a ficcari.
—Chi su' sti parulazzi?
Sapiti ben parrari.

—E vaja cu st'affruntu,
non fari la minchiuna,
ficcata la vurrissi
cu tutti li cugghiuna.

—Non chiù, pi caritati!
Chi cosa v'affirrau?
—Cazzissimu! Chi stizza!
To matri 'un ti parrau?

—Me matri 'un dissi autru:
Figghia, non t'affruntari,
e zoccu ti dicissi
tu mai divi niari.

Now let my hands at last
your lovely teats caress
and let my eager mouth
your nipples suck and kiss."

"What kind of talk is this?
Oh Lord, I'm so ashamed!
Stop reaching with your hands,
and let go of my breasts."

"If I touch your sweet breasts,
my dick becomes erect.
Nice, give me your hand.
You see, how straight it stands?"

"O my, what a long thing!
What is this thing so taut?"
"Turn 'round and lift your legs
and pull up your nightgown.

This thing is meant to go
inside your little pussy."
"What ugly words you're using.
You should know better manners."

"Come now. Stop playing shy.
Don't be a hypocrite!
You probably would like
to swallow my balls, too."

"Please stop, I beg of you!
What's wrong with you tonight?"
"Goldarn it! I'm pissed off!
Your mother didn't explain?"

"She simply said to me:
My daughter, don't be bashful!
No matter what he he asks,
you're never to say no."

—Sti chiacchiri lassamu,
ca chiù non pozzu stari.
Rapi li cosci, allentati,
mi sentu siddiari.

—Gnurnò, non vi siddiati,
scantari mi faciti,
li cosci vi li rapu,
fazzu zoccu diciti.

—Chiddu chi a tia ti fazzu
ora li vidirai.
Chi gustu dilicatu,
o Nici, pruvirai!

—Di supra m'acchianastivu.
Vivih quantu pisati!
Chi è sta cosa dura
ca cca m'appuntiddati?

Matruzza mia, unni siti,
pirchì non m'aiutati,
di sutta stu maceddu
pirchì non mi livati?

—Strìnciti li dintuzzi,
tanticchia di pacenza,
non ti la ficcu tutta
ma ti ni ficcu menza.

E comu tutta chista
vuliti cca 'nficcari
ntra un purtusiddu nicu
ch'è quantu un ghiditali?

— Ora ti fazzu vidiri
si tutta 'un ti la trasu,
cu quattru botti fermi
vidi comu la 'ncasu.

"So let us stop this talk.
I can't take any more.
Open your legs, relax,
I'm really getting mad."

"Oh no, please, there's no need,
you're scaring me a bit.
I'll open up my legs.
and your commands I'll heed."

"What I demand from you,
you will find out at once.
What delicate sweet taste,
o Nice, you will feel."

"You've climbed on top of me.
O my! You are so heavy.
What is that long, hard thing
you're pressing against me?

Dear Mother, where are you?
Why don't you help me now?
Why don't you rescue me
from this harsh slaughtering?"

"A little patience, dear!
Just clench your teeth a bit.
I won't go all the way,
I'll put it half way in."

"How can you drive that thing
inside of me complete?
Inside a little hole
no bigger than a thimble?"

"Now I will show you how.
I'll drive it all inside
with just a few deft shots.
You'll see, I'll drive it home."

— Chi siti nfuriatu,
chi scossi chi mi dati...
ahi! curuzzu miu,
ssi pila mi tirati...

Vivih! comu mi trasi,
china di sangu sugnu!
Livativi di supra
ca tuttu vi sgranfugnu!

Vaia, ca chiù di menza
ti n'haiu già nficcatu,
già ti cumincia a piaciri,
mumentu furtunatu.

Vasami nta la vucca
ca già staju ittannu...
lu sticchiu ncugna a mia,
e vammi cazziannu..

Chi è sta cosa cauda
ca tutta m'arricriati?
Mi piaci picca picca,
faciti, sicutati...

Non ti lu dissi o Nici
ca piaciri t'avria?
Vidi sidd'è minsogna
chiddu ca ti dicia.

Ma vui pirchì allintati?
Chiù forza non aviti?
Vaja, n'autru tanticchia,
chiù dintra la trasiti.

— Dimmi la viritati:
è gustu dilicatu?
Forza, curuzzu miu,
m'inforza già lu ciatu.

"Oh please, don't push so hard!
Your blows are killing me.
You're pulling out my hair,
you are too wild, my dear!

You're in, my God, but how?
I'm full of blood down there!
Get off of me right now,
or else I'll scratch your face!"

"I'm more than half way in.
Come on, don't make me stop.
You're starting to enjoy it,
this is the best of times.

So kiss me in the mouth,
for I'm about to come.
Your pussy push against me
and let me fuck you hard."

"What is this warmth I feel,
that's giving me such pleasure?
I'm starting to enjoy
this thing. Keep doing it."

"Did I not tell you, Nice,
that you would grow to like it.
You see I was not lying
when I was telling you."

"But why have you slowed down?
Your strength has ebbed away.
Come on, a little more
and you'll be all inside."

"Tell me the truth, my love,
is this not a sweet taste?
Let's try again, my love,
my strength is coming back."

— A dirivi lu veru,
di novu lu faria,
pirchì chiù soddisfatta
allura ristiria.

— Ed iu pri cuntintariti
di novu ti la nficcu,
pirchì di stu negoziu
ni sugnu veru liccu.

Li ciati già s'avanzanu,
curcativi, nfurzati,
mi sentu iri in estasi
mentri chi vui cazziati.

Non chiù? ci ripusamu?...
Chi gustu dilicatu!
Ma tantu sudisfatta
non haiu già ristatu.

Di novu lu faria,
si vui ci accunsintiti.
Ficcatimilla prestu,
chiù tempu non pirditi.

Ed iu pri cuntintariti
di novu ti la chiantu.
Te ccà sti dui minchiati
e sazziati frattantu.

A chiddu ca ora viju
nni sì troppu guluta.
E dillu ch'arraggiavi
pri essiri futtuta.

"To tell the truth of it,
I'd like to do it over,
because I am convinced
I'll be more satisfied."

"And I, to make you happy,
will stick it in again,
because I am quite fond
of this sweet business."

"Our breathing is now faster,
bend down and put more pressure.
I feel such ecstasy
as you are fucking me.

You're stopping? Are we resting?
What delicate new taste!
But I, to tell the truth,
am not yet satisfied.

If it's all right, I think,
I'd like to try again.
So, shove it deep inside,
don't waste any more time."

"And I, to make you happy,
will be glad to comply.
Here take a few more shots
and let these be enough.

As I can tell already,
you're something of a glutton.
You — there's no need to lie —
were dying to get laid."

Fillidi

Su vivu pri miraculu,
Iu giù muria annigatu;
Chistu n'è sticchiu, o Fillidi,
Si chiama purticatu.

Si prima di lu coitu
Tu mi l 'avissi dittu,
Iu cci puteva trasiri
'Ncarrozza rittu rittu.

E assisu comu un principi,
Di chiddu ccu li ciaffi,
Mi cci mitteva a curriri
Senza pigghiari scaffi.

Si mai cridia truvarisi
In tia vucca d'infernu,
Mi dispunia a tummaricci
Nostanti ch'era invernu.

Quannu, 'ntra ssa voragini
Lu cazzu iu vitti immersu,
Dicia fra me medesimu:
Addiu, lu cazzu è persu!

Quant'è ssu sticchiu! Ah Fillidi,
Tu pri suverchiu cunnu
Non cunti 'ntra li fimmini,
Sì morta pri stu munnu.

Si chiddu non poi sentiri
Gustusu, 'nzuccaratu
Piaciri, chi pò nasciri
Da un cazzu 'nsiiddatu.

Phyllis

A wonder I'm alive!
I almost drowned down there!
That's not a pussy, Phyllis!
Yours is a thoroughfare!

If you had told me that,
when we began to screw,
I could have entered you
straight with my coach and hat

and sitting like a prince
and not one who's a chump,
I would have started running,
without concern for bumps.

If I believed I'd find
the mouth of hell in you,
I would have said adieu,
though it was winter time.

When I saw my poor cock
immersed in your abyss,
I kept repeating this:
Adieu, my cock is lost!

What a huge pussy, Phyllis!
Because it's oversized
you're not of womankind:
you should be eulogized!

If you can't feel the pleasure,
so sweet, so true, so great,
that a well-saddled cock
is bound to generate,

Vurissi pr'arraspariti
Ssi turgidi membrani
Non minchi a coddu d'uteri,
Ma culumbrini sani.

Pri mia non sò truvaricci
Non versu e nuddu situ,
E mancu a pascipecura
Ca stringi qualchi ghitu.

Pri lu disiu cci arrisicu.
Trasu lu cazzu invanu;
Cci arrunzu appressu, e sciddicu
E mi nni vaju sanu.

Cui si putia supponiri
Truvari ssa largura
In tia, chi sì nna giuvina
Di picciula figura?

Si tratta ca stu manicu
Scarsu non è, sebbeni
Suffertu ha milli trivuli,
Ma 'ngrassa 'ntra li peni.

Cridia farmi la guaddira,
E trasiri ccu stentu,
Non dimenarmi all'aria,
E futtiri a lu ventu.

Sticca di vinti pollici
D'un patri zucculanti
Chi penni, sbatti e sventula,
Perciò refrigeranti;

Stu pezzu magnatiziu,
Chi snoda argiutu e feru
Lu so alaterio, e in furia
Straggi minaccia alteru;

you need, to scratch your itch,
not uterus-shaped dicks,
to fill that gulf-wide ditch,
you need large, rounded pricks!

For me, it's not a cinch.
The way I cannot find,
not even from behind,
which tightens it an inch.

In yearning for the hole,
I stick my dick inside,
but I just slip and slide,
and I am swallowed whole.

Whoever would have dreamed
that a young girl like you,
with such a tiny frame,
could have an avenue!

And it cannot be said
my cock's too small to please.
Though it has had it bad,
it's grown in size with woes.

I thought that from the strain
a hernia I'd get,
not wriggle there in vain
and fuck the wind and sweat.

This twenty-inches thing,
like that of monks who wear
sandals, that's free to swing
and hang, cooled by the air;

This princely business,
which shows itself a master,
with pride and haughtiness,
and threatens wide disaster,

Vidrai ccu tò spittaculu
Trasiri linnu e stancu;
T'arrivirà all'esofagu,
Senza tuccari un quancu.

In menzu a tantu vacuu
Sarà, in manera strana,
In locu di prepuziu
Battagghiu di campana.

E un qualchi rifrigeriu
Sulu putrai pruvari
Quannu un cazzu a martoriu
Dda dintra poi sunari.

Ma, dimmi, Filli, in grazia,
Chi lima è stata chissa
Perenni ed instancabili,
Ca t'allargau la fissa?

Non sai chi sì in piriculu,
Chi pò a lu funnamentu
Lu sticchiu un ghiornu unirisi
Pri tantu smanciamentu?

E allura, oh chi disgrazia!
Si forma nna vanedda,
Da cui pò sdivacarisi
La matri e li vudedda.

Amica, ti ringraziu,
Ti ristirò obbligatu,
Oh quantu! Diu pirdunati
Lu scantu ca m'hai datu.

you'll see, as in a skit,
as it goes straight and true,
reaching your stomach pit,
while never touching you.

nside so great a void,
instead of as a stopper,
my dick could be employed
inside a bell as clapper.

And you will find relief,
perhaps, when a man's cock
will toll to mourn with grief
for someone's funeral.

Pray tell, what kind of file,
Phyllis, so true and tried,
so tireless and virile,
wore out your hole so wide?

I hope you are aware
your pussy and your ass,
through all the wear and tear,
will fuse as one, alas!

And then, oh, what a mess!
a pathway would be formed
through which would find egress
your uterus and stomach.

I want to thank you, love.
I'm grateful, to be fair.
But I must say, by Jove,
you gave me quite a scare.

Clori

Non negu ca li fimmini
Amanu cazzu grossu
E longo, e latu, e turgidu,
E duru comu un ossu.

Ma chissa tua è culovria,
E' sugghiu di tilaru,
E' cosa di spittaculu.
Tirsi, non cc'è riparu.

La testa di ssa pifera
Sula, senza lu restu,
Non sulamenti sazia,
Ma ancora fa 'ndiggestu.

Voi di ssu cazzu barbaru
Ca sia nna cosa magna
Prova chiù indubitabili ?
Nna donna si nni lagna.

Quannu trasiu 'ntra l'uteru
Ssa furma d'allargari,
mi fici, oimè, contorciri.
Mi vinni di cacari.

M'arriminau li visceri,
'Ntisi squarciati a brani
L'ovara, la clitoridi,
Li tubbi fallopiani.

Ccu ssa gran torcia in gremiu
Mi parsi ch'era prena:
Li dogghi già mi vinniru,
E mi mancau la lena.

Chloris

I really can't deny
that girls love a big dick
that's long, and fat and spry,
and harder than a brick,

but yours is a python,
it is a ceiling beam,
a show, a real tragedian!
Tirsis, yours is extreme!

The head alone, without
the rest, of your big bastion,
not only satisfies,
but gives one indigestion.

Your dick is quite incredible.
I offer you a proof
that is incontrovertible:
women will voice reproof.

When in my uterus
you drove your stretching tool,
it caused a barbarous
urge to expell my stool.

It caused womb injuries,
it diced in little cubes
my clit and ovaries
and my Fallopian tubes.

With such a heavy torch
I thought I was with child,
felt labor pains approach
and then went limp awhile.

Mi ricercau ogni latebra,
Mi fici certa ghiotta.
Ch'iu già esalava l'anima,
Muria sutta la botta.

In ogni corpu validu
Chi dava all'intestini
Ssa catapulta orribili,
S'aprevanu li rini.

Si sburdì ogni veiculu,
L'uretra si sbisazza,
Sgurgari vulia a profluviu,
Nè potti la pisciazza.

Ma, Tirsi, a chi può serviri
Ssu gran minchiuni tò?
E' certu ca pri futtiri
Giuvari non ti può.

O di carrozza mettilu,
Ch'è giustu, pri timuni;
O megghiu fà, appuntiddalu
Pri stanga di purtuni.

Aletta, è veru, un'anima
Nna minchia di li vaschi,
Ma no nna spranga elettrica
Ca nesci di li naschi.

Sia grossu, sia maiusculu
Un cazzu, a tutti piaci,
Ognuna lu desidera,
Fa sputazzedda, e taci.

Ognuna si nni giubila
D'un cazzu chi non stanca.
Ma poi detesta ed odia
Un cugnu chi sbalanca.

It filled each nook, each hole,
it gave me such a glut,
I nearly lost my soul
and died from the assault.

With every new insult
that you drove deep inside,
your horrid catapult
my kidneys opened wide.

With all resistance gone
and my urethra blown,
the urine sought to flow,
but had nowhere to go.

Say, Tirsis, what's it for?
How can you use your cock?
It can't be used to fuck,
of that I am quite sure.

So put it in a car
and use it as a shaft,
or as a handle bar,
or rudder on a raft.

A soul gets much delight
from seeing a huge dick,
but not from such a stick
that makes electric light.

So everyone enjoys
a dick that's big and strong.
It's every woman's joy:
She spits and goes along.

Each woman celebrates
a dick that knows no rest,
but she detests and hates
a wedge she can't ingest.

Nè giusta cosa parimi
Fari a nna pasturedda
Nna leva matematica
ccu ssa gran manuedda.

Ch'è grossu, ch'è spropositu!
Ch'è longu, matri mia!
Pri misurarlu a pollici
La manu stanchiria.

Ch'è duru, ch'è insoffribili!
E quannu, oddiu, si carca.
Si fa ostinatu ed empiu.
Pari un eresiarca.

Nna vecchia ottagenaria
Chi nta nn'oscura cava
Havi un sticchiazzu fracitu
Di pistilenti bava;

Chi giaci fra l'inerzia
Allaccaratu e spanu,
E l'anni e li disgrazii
Lu prolungaru all'anu.

S'in chista va ad immergirlu,
Fissura orrenda e lasca,
Dirria doppu li spasimi:
Gesuzzu, focu e frasca!

Pri lu conatu insolitu
Già m'allascai di sutta;
Nè foru suli pidita,
Iu m'allurdavi tutta.

D'una minchiazza simili
Scanzari Diu nni pozza,
Minchia ca fa stravidiri,
E tocca ccu la vozza.

It seems to me unjust,
if I can be quite frank,
to use that monstrous crank
for a maid-lifting test.

It's an unseemly gland!
How big and long, my Lord!
To measure it by hand,
the mind would grow too bored!

How hard, insufferable!
And when inside, what lunatic,
how evil and unbearable!
It's probably a heretic!

An old octagenarian
who lives in caves, meantime,
and whose old pussy reeks
with oozing and foul slime,

which slowly wastes away
in rotten disarray,
and which through age and woes
with her ass has been fused,

if in this horrid fissure
you plunged your mighty prier,
she'd say, after the torture
Oh Jesus, I'm on fire!

For the uncommon urge
I soiled my bottom parts.
It was a mighty purge,
nor was it only farts.

God spare us from such dicks
the likes of yours, I pray!
that on your eyes play tricks
and make you go astray.

Chi mai non ci putissiru
'Ncappari cristiani;
Anzi chiuttostu vidirla
In vucca di li cani.

Pri mia, Tirsi, ristarimi
Celibi mi delibru,
Simmai ogni prepuziu
Sarria di ssu calibru.

Sarria pri non suffririmi
In senu ssa baruffa
Cuntenta di ristarimi
Lu sticchiu ccu la muffa.

Và! e quannu tu voi futtiri
Abbuscati nna donna
Ca sia capaci a ghiuttirsi
In gremmu ssa colonna.

E siddu un Sticchiu simili
Può darsi 'ntra lu munnu,
Allura putrà dirisi
Ca na caverna è un cunnu.

Ccu mia ssa canna d'organu
Chiù non farà sunata;
Lu celu mi nni liberi !
Nni restu azzaccagnata.

Cadivi 'ntra la trappula
Sta vota, accussì fu:
E' rossu st'occhiu? Allargati,
Tu nun mi 'ncocci chiù.

No Christian should fall prey
to it in her lifetime.
It should be thrown, I say,
into the mouths of dogs.

And, Tirsis, as for me,
I'd choose to remain chaste
if every dick would be
the same size as your beast.

So as not to endure
that thing inside of me,
but keep my pussy free,
I'd let the mold mature.

Go! When you want to screw,
go look for someone new:
a woman who can swallow
your column in her hollow.

And if in man's enclave
a cunt like that exists,
it can be said, at least,
a pussy is a cave.

In me, your organ pipe
will not sound causing strife.
Lord, free me from your type.
I'd be fucked up for life.

I fell into your snare
this time! It's sad, but true.
Am I upset? Beware!
I'll never fuck with you!

Giuseppe Marco Calvino

Giuseppe Marco Calvino

Lu Futtituri Filosofu

Pri mia nun ci su beddi,
Pri mia nun ci su brutti,
Abbasta chi si futti,
E poi cu cui è è.

Lu cazzu 'unn'havi oricchi,
Nun havi nasu ed occhi,
Basta chi lu 'ncrafocchi,
E poi comu è è.

Cu scarpi e senza scarpi,
Cu fauda o cu vistina,
Cu scialla o mantillina,
L'afferru, e 'un guardu cchiù

Facissi fetu o ciauru,
Pri mia sempri è la stissa;
Si fa ciauru di fissa
Nun nni pretennu cchiù.

Quannu la spogghiu nuda,
Qualunqui cacazzara
Diventa cosa rara,
E sia comu è è.

Diventa 'na rigina!
Chi a mia mi basta sulu
Chi avissi sticchiu e culu,
E scialu unni iè iè.

Li minni cci li vogghiu:
Ma sianu grossi o nichi,
Basta chi ti cci strichi,
Chi sempri minni sù.

The Fucking Philosopher

There are no pretty women,
there are no ugly women,
as long as I can screw,
it matters not with who.

A dick does not have ears,
it has no nose or eyes,
as long as it can burrow,
it cares not for tomorrow.

Wearing a skirt or dress,
with shawls or with much less,
with shoes or with a cape,
I grab her by the nape.

If she smells foul or sweet,
for me it's just a treat.
If she but smells of game,
for me she is fair game.

When I start to undress them
any old cunt at all
becomes a precious gem
and then I have a ball.

She grows into a Queen
for all I ever want,
to make my pleasure keen,
is just an ass and cunt.

Teats are for me a must!
They can be big or small,
for when I squeeze a bust
I'm not concerned at all.

Qualunqui nazioni,
Sia turca, sia cinisa,
Quann'è senza cammisa
Fussi di lu Perù.

Sia bianca, russa, niura,
Qualunqui sia culuri,
S'avi li carni duri,
Si fussi anchi lillà.

Mi piaci si cazzia,
Mi piaci si 'un si movi,
Comu la trovi trovi,
E soccu ti fa fa.

Mi piaci a pascipecura
Mi piaci a 'ngrasciaspitu,
A scarrica marito,
Comu cchiù megghiu pò.

Sia 'ncammara, 'ncucina,
'Ncampagna, 'ntra li strati,
Abbasta chi chiavati,
E sia sutta un burò.

Sia virgini, figghiata,
L'avissi largu o strittu...
La minchia, quannu arrittu,
Chi cumpassia quant'è?

O fussi longa o curta,
O fussi grassa o sicca,
Basta chi si cci ficca,
E poi comu è è.

Picciotti, lu cunfessu,
Sugnu c'un sensu sulu,
E avennu sticchiu e culu,
Nun sentu passidda.

Their countries may be close,
far China or Rangoon,
but when they're without clothes,
they could be from the Moon.

She can be white or red,
or black of any hue;
if she is good in bed,
she can be purple too.

I like them if they move,
I like them if they don't.
As long as I can groove,
they can do what they want.

I take them like sheep-grazing,
or simply husband-cruising.
I like them from behind
or any way I find.

In bedrooms or the zoo,
in kitchens, open air;
as long as one can screw,
it does not matter where.

She can be tight or wide,
a virgin or a mother,
for when my dick's wide-eyed,
with measures it won't bother.

She can be tall or short,
she can be fat or thin.
If I can put it in,
it makes for perfect sport.

My friends I must confess,
I have only one sense,
and having cunt and ass,
I seek no other ends.

L'occhi appena si 'mpannanu,
La vucca si 'nsirragghia,
Cumincia la battaglia,
E affunciu unni va va.

E' certu chi la bedda
E' un corpu di furtuna!
Ma abbutta li cugghiuna
Ddu 'ncripativu no.

La voli dintra l'arma,
E intantu la rifiuta;
S'arriffa tutta, sputa,
Vi giura chi nun pò.

Eppuru cc'è a cui piacinu,
Tutti ssi sicchi micchi...
Ma chi? ciauru di sticchi
Nun sannu chi cos'è.

Ammaluccuti accuccanu,
Alliccanu, pilliccanu;
Ma po' forsi chi ficcanu?
Ma sticchiu chi cci nn'è?
Amuri, sintimentu,

E 'un si cci arriva mai...
Si la tuccati, ahi! ahi!
Lu solitu nun pò.

V'arrobbanu, vi spogghianu,
Vi portanu a 'nfuddiri,
Po' sempri senti diri
Chiddu ffuttutu no.

Ci piaci e si nni prejanu
Ssa facci cadaverica,
Chi futti cu la sterica
Chiamannu a so mamà.

My eyes are getting cloudy,
my teeth are tightly clenched,
the battle's growing rowdy,
my lips kiss the first wench.

Fair women are for sure
a stroke of luck it's true,
but nothing I hate more
than women who won't screw.

They want it in their souls,
but always they refuse;
they spit, they thumb their noses,
and swear that they can't ball.

And yet some men enjoy
such women's wily ploys,
but they don't know the joy
a pussy smell deploys.

Like dumbbells, hockeypucks,
they flirt their heart's content,
but do you think they fuck?
Of pussies not a hint!

There's love there's sentiment,
but they will get nowhere
for if you touch them there
as usual they can't!

They steal your soul away,
they drive you quite insane,
but all you hear them say
is no, no, no, again!

Men love her pale complexion,
they're giddy with delight,
but when it's time for action,
she calls out for her mother.

Vonnu la titulata,
Vonnu la barunissa
Pri tantu poi di fissa
La fannu a tu pri tu.

Tutti profumi e ciauri,
Tutti galantaria...
Ma poi 'na camurria,
E 'un sannu comu fu.

Na signuruzza nobili
'Mpistata, 'unn'è possibili!
'Nn è cosa presumibili!
E 'un sannu chi cos'è.

'Mpuddi, talori, pertichi,
Fitti chi 'n ponnu agghiuttiri
Si vannu a fari futtiri,
E 'un sannu chi cos'è.

O curtigghiari bacchiari!
Ciatu di l'arma mia!
Oh comu m'arricria
Ddu vostru prontu si!

Tu nobili! tu bedda!
Tu duci cchiù di tutti,
O tu chi ti strafutti
Pri un miseru tarì!

La simplici natura
Tu sula la conosci:
Basta chi ti l'arrusci,
E poi cu cui è è!...

Pri mia si siti beddi,
Pri mia si siti brutti,
Basta chi si strafutti,
E poi comu è è.

Nobility men stress:
they want a baroness!
But when it's time to screw,
their hands will have to do.

Oh what perfumes, what smells!
All gallantry and airs!
Men then get gonorrhea
and they don't know from where.

From such nobilities
how can you get VD?
It's an impossibility!
They don't know what it is.

Boils, rashes and things swell,
when swallowing there's pain,
and men go down to hell,
unable to explain.

Sweet women, I confess,
you are my breath and joy!
How much do I enjoy
your ever ready yes!

You're noble, you're the best,
much sweeter than the rest,
you who give queenly fucks,
not even for two bucks.

You are the only ones
who answer nature's call.
As long as you get boned,
you'll screw with one and all

If you are fair it's fine
if ugly it's fine too.
As long as I can screw
it does not matter who!

Lu Filosofu Pintutu

Addiu cazzu, addiu culu, ed addiu sticchiu!
Vogghiu fari 'na vita ritirata;
Voggh'essiri la corda cu lu sicchiu
Cu dda fissa, chi Diu m'ha distinata.
Promettu e giuru a ssu sulu virticchiu
Fidi in eternu sta santa jurnata;
Chi pozz'essiri surdu, ciuncu e mutu,
Si sti cugghiuna nun ci appennu in vutu.

Abbannunu lu culu schifiusu;
Sù statu un porcu, sù statu un vastasu.
Ddu cazzu chi niscia tuttu lippusu!
Lu fetu a la nisciuta di ddu vasu!...
Ma monaci e parrini?... ci hannu l'usu;
Ci l'hanno assuefattu ora lu nasu.
Comu! ficcarla unni si va di corpu?
Oh comu ci pirdia l'arma e lu corpu!

Mi sia tuttu lu munnu tistimoniu
Di sta me firma risoluzioni,
Comu un cani arraggiassi lu dimoniu.
Un cazzu! mancu pri tantazioni.
Futtu, ma cu lu santu matrimoniu,
E cu dda santa binidizioni;
E speru sempri d'aviri presenti,
Ch'è unu di li setti sagramenti.

D'ora 'nnavanti muggheri e maritu.
Finiu: nun c'è baascia chi mi 'ncappa.
E futtiremu secunnu lu ritu,
Idest, comu si dici, a ficu a chiappa.
Pasci-pecura, a ponti, a 'ngrascia-spitu...
Mai mai: si poi lu quagghiu si nni scappa?
Minchiuni! si va 'nterra chi delittu!
Cosa di cazzu! L'omu è malidittu!

The Reformed Philosopher

Goodbye cock, goodbye ass, sweet pussy, goodbye!
I want to start a different life today.
Like wick in candle wax I aim to be
with that sweet pussy God has granted me.
I promise to be true this holy day
to that sweet hole alone and never stray!
I'll hang my balls upon a wall as vow,
or else strike me deaf, dumb and lame, right now!

I hereby do forsake the filthy ass!
I've been a swine, an awful worthless pig!
That dick emerging full of grime, alas!
The awful smell emerging from that dig!
So what about the monks and priests? I think
their noses are accustomed to the stink.
Imagine! Sticking it where people shit!
Oh how I gave my soul and flesh for it!

I call upon the universe to see
this firm and most unyielding resolution,
and may the devil burst most angrily!
With all my might I will resist temptation.
I'll fuck but within blessed matrimony
and with our Lord's most holy benediction!
I must remember as I drive the rod
it's one of seven sacraments of God.

Husband and wife henceforth, just me and you.
It's over! No more trollops there to sway me.
And in accordance with the rite we'll screw.
No weird positions: the married couple's way
no sheep-a-grazing, no more doggy style.
Never again! What if sperm leaked meanwhile
and trickled to the floor? Oh blasphemy!
Man would be damned thoughout eternity!

Minchiuni chiddu nescila a lu puntu,
Pirchì a 'mprinari nun ci fussi scantu!
Oh quantu armuzzi, si fazzu lu cuntu,
Oh quantu armuzzi 'ntra lu limmu santu!
Ora, fatta la cruci, appena muntu,
Forti chi la cafuddu, e chi la chiantu,
Ad procreandum, nun mi catamiu,
A estinguendam libidinem, e finiu.

Ddi manu 'nculu, cu ddu iditeddu
Chi tillica, chi stuzzica e cattigghia,
Finiu: li manu supra un ghiumazzeddu,
E comu la mudestia nni cunsigghia.
Misu a ddi minni comu lu viteddu,
Finiu: basta chi trasi la cavigghia,
Ussu tu, jesu jesu, adaciu adaciu,
Lu cchiù cchiù mi permettu qualchi baciu.

Anzi stu baciu chi si dassi 'nfrunti,
Vasannu comu carni vattiata.
Sucuna, lingua e lingua e dd'autri cunti,
Dddi muzzicuna di n'arma arraggiata,
Ddu funciari 'ntra ddi minni junti,
Comu si si farria la sapunata,
L'ucchiazzi chi si mancianu la terra,
Mai, musiddu strittu, e l'occhi 'nterra.

Mugghieri mia, bisogna chi t'arrizzu;
Pri sarvarimi 'un c'è nudd'autru mezzu.
Avi assai chi lu munnu scannalizzu.
Lu diavulu cc'è statu pri lu mezzu.
Futtemu: ma li jorna di sirvizzu,
Li festi 'un si nni parla, nun c'è mezzu.
Poi si ti fai lu cuntu ci guadagni,
S'è pri tia sulu, nn'avirrai cumpagni.

Pacenza: è veru, comu ti 'nsignai
Tutti ddi jochi 'un li faremu cchiui:
Ma cazzu! siquitannu c'era guaj;

How stupid to pull out before I came
for fear of pregnancies! How can I count
how many little souls without a name
were sent to limbo all on my account?
Now having crossed myself and climbed on you
I'll stick it deep inside and start to screw
without much worrying for procreation,
until lust runs its course to the end station.

No middle finger to insinuate and tease
or titillate; no hands upon your ass!
No more! Hands on your hairy mound? No, please!
We'll heed the rules of modesty, alas!
No hanging from your teats like a young bull!
No more! If I can dip my carrot full
and slowly move without much fuss or stress...
The most I will allow is a chaste kiss.

In fact, upon your forehead I would place
the chastest kiss as would a catholic.
No sucking tongues in mouth and face to face;
No biting like a raving lunatic,
no smacking of wet lips upon joined teats,
producing soap sufficient to wash clothes,
no crazy eyes that stare the ground below!
No more! Tight lips and keep your eyes low.

I have to take corrective measures, wife!
I've scandalized the world for far too long.
There is no other way to save my life.
The devil is to blame! I can't be wrong!
Let's screw, but only during working days,
and let us then abstain on holidays.
But this is your big gain, are you aware?
My dick will be all yours! You will not share.

Patience! It's true that we will never play
all of the games I taught you oh so well.
But shit! If we continued, we would have to pay.

Sarriamu a casa cauda tutti dui.
Munciri li cugghiuna? senza mai!
Sucariti la minchia?... un cazzu... a cui!...
Basari sticchiu, alliccari... minchiuni!...
Matri mia, chi schifiu!... chi piccatuni!...

Mutamu vita: masinnò a dda banna
Nni fuchianu lu culu, gioia mia.
L'ucchiuzzi 'nterra, lu coddu a la banna.
E sai chi cosa ti cunsigghirria?
'Ntra li cammisi giustu 'nta dda banna
Ci fai un pirtusu, e tattu 'un ci nni sia:
Stu rimediu truvau certu Baruni
Chi futtia la mugghieri a dinucchiuni.

Cussì niscennu lu memmaru sulu,
'Mmezzu di la spaccazza ti lu 'nfilu;
Cussì 'un c'è scantu chi pozz'iri 'nculu,
Chi sennu allatu vinirria lu sfilu.
E poi, 'nfia chi 'un finisci lu perculu,
Saria indecenza stari a pilu e pilu...
Si, d'oggi 'nnanzi vogghiu chi s'avvezza
A maniarimilla cu la pezza.

Anchi pisciannu, sempri la cammisa:
Chi tanti voti la bestia ffuttuta
Senti appena li jdita ed attisa,
E quantu la viditi 'ncazzunuta!
E po' chi testa quannu pigghia 'mprisa!
Chi senti capizzuni? chi m'ascuta?
Lu cchiù tintu di jornu; chi di notti
L'è finutu, c'è datu quattru botti.

Ma di jornu, di jornu cu ddu bozzu!...
Cu è chi 'un si nni adduna ch'è lu cazzu?
Tant'è, 'un lu sannu tutti chi 'un ci pozzu;
Figurati chi sorti di 'mmarazzu?
Viu li pirsuni, e mi votu lu cozzu;
Ed assicuratillu mi nni fazzu:

We would have ended up in burning Hell.
Squeezing my balls? Don't even think of it!
Sucking my cock? Not mine, no more! Like shit!
Kissing your pussy, licking my big dick?
Oh Christ! An awful sin, a dirty trick!

Let's change our ways or else down there, my love,
they'll set our asses on a burning stove!
Keep looking to the side with your eyes down
and here is something else that I suggest:
cut holes in every nightgown that you own
so contact is avoided. That is best!
A baron found this clever remedy
and he would screw his wife upon one knee.

This way by simply taking out my cock
I'll shove it into your portentous crack
without the fear that I would screw your ass,
which being close, would be hard to resist.
And then, besides the danger that we'd face,
joining of pubic hairs would not take place.
Henceforth, I want it to get used, my love,
to being always handled with a glove.

So when I pee I will use my shirt tip,
for many times this fucking little beast,
feeling my fingers right away perks up
and it's erect and ready for the feast!
And then what stubbornness, how proud it stands!
You think it feels the reins? Or heed commands?
In day time it is bad. It gives me woes!
At nighttime a few shots and down it goes.

But in day time with that bulge in my pants...!
who would not know its nature, save a fool?
I try to thwart it but I simply can't.
Imagine the embarassment I feel?
When I see people I just turn my back
in vain attempts to cover up that sack.

Ssu diavulu, ssa gran tintazioni,
Chissa mi porta a la pirdizioni.

Basta; d'ora nn'avanzi nautra vita;
E speru chi livannu sta tuccata,
La vidirremu 'na santa rumita
'Ntra lu so cappucceddu ritirata.
Vidennu a tia 'na santa Margarita
Avi a sentiri anch'idda la chiamata.
Addiu, munnazzu, addiu ti lassu tuttu,
Basta chi sarvu l'arma, e mi nni futtu.

Lu Filosofu Minaturi

Mentri chi opera
La fantasia,
0 Lici bacchiara
Si sempri mia.

Tutti ssi lastimi,
Ssu 'un vogghiu e da
Tutti ssi smorfi
Di to mamà,

Tutti sù inutili,
Ss'aria, ssi sfrazzi
Si voggiu futtiri,
Sù tutti cazzi.

Qualunqui fimmina,
Sia 'na rigina,
Cedi a un filosofu
Chi si la mina.

L'ossa ruditivi,
Cani gilusi,
Vi futtu l'anima
Cu l'occhi chiusi.

That awful devil, oh that great temptation!
Pussies will lead me straight to my perdition.

Henceforth, I want to lead another life.
Enough! And leaving out this final bout,
I see my dick a hermit far from strife,
wearing a hood above its head, that lout!
Since you've become a saintly Margaret,
it too might be inclined to make your bet.
Goodbye mean world, goodbye, I leave you all!
To hell with you, I want to save my soul!

The Masturbating Philosopher

While my imagination
is busily at work,
for you there's no salvation,
fair Lici, you are mine!

Your many dumb complaints
your ever ready no's,
all the vain gesturing
even your mother knows,

are no defense for you.
Your airs and haughtiness,
if I decide to screw,
could not mean any less.

No woman can fight off,
no queen is queen enough,
a mighty *philosophe*
who knows how to jerk off.

You jealous little bitches,
in your own juices stew!
For when I close my eyes
your souls I'm free to screw!

Mentri chi opera
La fantasia,
E quali fimmina
Mi scappirria?...

Giovi chi vantanu
Gran futtituri
Criu ch'appi ad essiri
Gran minaturi!

Criu cchiù probabili
Si la minassi,
Ch'in crastu o in tauru
Si trasformassi.

Tutti ddi strucciuli,
Dda pioggia d'oru,
Di un cazzu all'aria
Li sgricci foru.

Chi turri e cammari
Di brunzu e ferru!
Fussi 'ntra ll'aria,
Puru l'afferru.

Quant'è ridiculu
Ddu gran signuri:
Cc'è eunuchi e buzzari
Pri un minaturi?

Chi cc'è sirragghiu,
Chi cc'è Sultanu
Pri l'omu liberu
Cu l'arti 'mmanu!

Di 'n'omu liberu,
Privatu e sulu
Divi guardarisi
Pri lu so culu.

While my imagination
is working busily
what woman in this nation
can ever flee from me?

I think that even Jove
that great old fornicator
more probably was just
a greater masturbator.

It's likely he jerked off,
as I have often thought,
instead of changing to
a bull or a he-goat.

That silly fairytale,
that mythic golden shower,
was nothing but the drops
from his dick's squirting power.

What chambers and what towers,
all made of bronze or steel!
If girls lived in the air,
I still would cop a feel!

How silly can he be
that wealthy eastern Prince!
Can fags and eunuchs be
from masturbators a defense?

Can there be any harems
or Sultans feel secure
when there is a free man
with hands as paramour?

And Sultans too must fear:
their ass is not their own
when there is a free man
with time who lives alone.

Basta chi opera
La fantasia,
Mi pozzu futtiri
'Na varvaria.

Forti chi un atomu
Lu senziu sferra
"Chi tirribiliu!
"Chi serra serra!

A panza all'aria
Pinsannu anticchia,
E Ciccia, e Paula,
Cocò, Maricchia,

Donna Virginia,
La Barunissa,
Tutti chi appuzzanu
Dannumi fissa!

Cui duna natichi,
Cui ammustra minni,
Carvaca l'autra,
Si chidda scinni.

Muncinu, strincinu,
Cazzianu, vasanu,
Trasinu, nescinu,
Ficcanu, 'ncasanu...

Tuttu ssu traficu,
Tutti ssi pidita?...
Cosa di sturdiri!...
Sti cincu jdita!...

Oh l'omu celebri
Chi la 'mmintau
E scuppulannula
Cci accuminzau!

While my mind is hard at work
there are no impediments!
With leisure I can fuck
an entire regiment.

It takes no time at all
to start the rolling ball,
then chaos breaks, pall-mall
and things begin to fall!

If I lie down
and start to think
Ciccia and Paula,
Cocò, Maricchia,

Lady Virginia,
the Baroness,
come give me pussy
and with largesse!

One gives me thighs,
her teats another,
one rides my dick,
after the other.

They grab and squeeze,
they kiss and hug,
they lick, theytease,
they plug, unplug...

All these festivities!
All these activities!
What great dexterities
in five extremities!

Praised be that famous man
who gave it origin,
the man who first began
by pulling on the foreskin.

Di la superbia
D'ogni baascia
Di la superbia
D'ogni bardascia.

L'orbi catolicu
Sarvau cu nenti,
L'orbi, pri futtiri
'Ntra peni e stenti!

E si nni dunanu
Pregi cchiù rari,
Putiri futtiri
Senza pagari?

Ora è probabili
Presunzioni
Chi 'unn'è antichissima
St'invinzioni.

S'era antichissima,
Forsi pri un pumu
L'umanu generi
Nun ghieva 'nfumu.

Gomorra e Sodoma
Pri lu pircocu
Nun subissavanu
Pioggi di focu.

Si un jornu Paridi
Si la minava,
Troja certissimu
Nun s'abbruciava.

Puru, guardannnusi
L'omu li manu
Duvia cumprenniri
Ssu granni arcanu

And from the haughty ploys
of every prostitute,
as from the haughtiness
of all the whoring boys,

the Christian universe,
which bore fate's awful curse,
to fuck in pain and strife
was thus made quickly safe.

And can there be
a greater treasure,
a rarer pleasure,
than to fuck free?

It's probably too bold-
a case of sheer presumption-
to think that this invention
is something that is very old.

For as I've always thought
it's likely the first couple
would not have come to naught
for tasting a sweet apple!

Gomorra, wicked Sodom
would not have gone to pot
with fire-raining problems
for tasting *apricot.*

If Paris on that day
had simply masturbated,
I am certain that old Troy
would not have been cremated.

Man, it would seem to me,
by looking at his hands,
this greatest mystery,
should have resolved at once.

Quannu la minchia
Tisa strincia.
'Ncoppula e scoppula...
Chi cci vulia?...

Solitu triulu
Di lu 'nvintari,
Ca doppu facili
La cosa pari.

Eu criu chi l'epoca
Sia da Colummu,
Quannu li pertichi
Vinniru 'nsummu.

Quannu ci vinniru
Da ddi paisi
Li ffuttutissimi
Mali francisi.

Li sticchi s'odianu,
E ognunu mina,
Quannu li vittiru
Cu la risina.

L'omu cu dubbiu
Di cafuddari,
Prima di trasila
Ci avrà a pinsari.

Ora la scoppula
Quasi chi chianta,
Ora la 'ncoppula
Pirchì si scanta,

Scoppula, 'ncoppula,
Rincuppulannu,
L'amicu Cesari
Si ja lanzannu.

Those hands that were clasped over
a cock that was erect.
Cover... uncover ...discover...
Not hard! Time to reflect...!

But that is where the trouble
with all inventions lies:
that after they're invented,
they all seem a child's play!

I think we must lay blame
to the Columbus age,
for that's when they first came
these boils that cause such rage.

That fucking malady,
men called the French disease,
was brought initially
from those new shores to these.

Men hated women's fluff
because they started oozing
and everyone jerked off
quite freely of their choosing.

The man who was afraid
to shove his dick inside
before he would get laid
would think and step aside.

At first he would uncap it
to put it into gear
but then he would recap it
in utter dread and fear.

Cover... uncover... cover
with all this covering,
our friend the Kaiser
grew hard and towering.

Eccu 'ntra un atomu
Cussì 'nvintata
L'arti utilissima
Di la minata.

L'arti chi 'mpregiu
Purtau lu cazzu,
E di li fimmini
Passau lu sfrazzu.

Gilusa furia
Pri idda taci,
Futtennu l'omini
In santa paci.

La mogghi a Tiziu,
La soru a Caju,
Ci futtu l'anima,
Ne passu un guaju.

'Mmezzu un gran populu,
Senz'autru stentu,
Misu 'ntra un angulu
Nni futtu centu.

Oh quantu è commodu
Ddu firriolu!
Passa 'na fimmina,
La futtu a volu.

Pri 'un dari scannalu
Cu la minata
C'è l'autra speci
Di la minata.

Gnuttica, sghiuttica,
Senza chi sbroccula,
Sulu li jdita
Fannu la gnoccula.

Without much hesitation
the very useful art
of manly masturbation
that moment had its start.

So there came forth an art
whereby men's dicks did gain
and which destroyed in part
the pussy long-lived reign.

No jealous fury burns
inside of men today.
In holy peace and quiet
they screw their days away.

Thus I am free to fuck
the wife of poor John Doe,
the sister of Joe Blow,
and not take chance on luck.

By sitting here alone,
or in a crowd's great bussle
a hundred girls I own
and fuck without a hassle.

Oh how convenient
this new expedient!
A woman passes by:
I fuck her on the fly.

But to avoid a scandal
with open masturbation,
we've found another handle:
a new way to jerk off.

By moving up and down
without uncovering;
letting the fingers do
all the maneuvering.

Fu di stu seculu
St'invinzioni,
Di un paraliticu
C'è opinioni.

Nun putia moviri
Lu ciuncu vrazzu,
Pollici ed indici
Muncia lu cazzu;

Tant'è, a l'immagini
Di sticchi e minni,
Conchiusi l'opera...
Cioè ci vinni.

E chi! a stu seculu
Li minaturi?
Assai chi un minanu
Cu lu vapuri.

Poi chistu è futtiri
Senz'autra pena:
Ch'è un santu futtiri
Quannu 'un si 'mprena.

'N'è, pisu inutili
Di società,
C'è cui bestemmia
A so papà!

Cui 'nterra semina
Dannatu è doppu...
Ma 'un c'è rimediu?...
'Na manu a coppu.

Natura provvida
A tutti nui
Nun fici ammatula
Li manu a dui.

In truth some people say
the guy who first began
this clever and new way
was a crippled man.

He could not move his arm
as it was stiff and numb,
but that did not disarm
his index and his thumb.

So as he concentrated
upon his pussy game,
his deed he terminated,
in short, he simply came.

So at the present day
the men who masturbate
are more, I vouch to say,
than those who fornicate.

With this there's no complaint:
this fucking's worry-free
and even somewhat saintly,
avoiding pregnancy.

Nor are there little ones,
a burden to the nation,
who curse their father's name
and their chance generation.

If you your semen spill
you will be damned to hell!
No way this to amend?
Just catch it with your hand!

Nature was generous:
a pair of useful hands
it gave to each of us.
That was part of the plans.

A lu manubriu
Una lavura,
L'autra a riciviri
La strincitura.

Tuttu è equilibriu,
Tuttu è previstu,
Era pri l'omini
Stu granni acquistu.

Lu seculu decimunonu

Seculu filosoficu!...
Seculu di stu cazzu...
Seculu minchiunissimu!
Seculu illuminatu!
Minchiuni! porcu! e pazzu!
Basta a diri stu seculu,
L'omu chi voli futtiri
Si chiama sciliratu.
Rubbari cu pulitica,
Nun è piccatu affattu:
Vinniri la giustizia
E' sociali pattu:
Ammazzari pri boria
Di li conquistaturi,
Ragiun di statu, gloria!
Cosi chi fannu onuri!
Scurciari anchi li poviri,
Drittu di proprietà:
Imposturari un miseru,
Geniu di verità.
Sulu sulu lu futtiri,
Chissu è piccatu sulu...
Tempi illuminatissimi!
Tempi di cazzi 'nculu!

One of the hands was meant
to hold our instrument,
the other was to gather
the squeezed and squirting lather.

All is in symmetry,
all things are pre-ordained;
for men's stability
this was a mighty gain.

The Nineteenth Century

A philosophical century!
A fucked up century indeed...
the dumbest century....
talk of Enlightenment!
Stupid filthy and crazy!
Suffice to say that in this century
the man who wants to fuck
is called disgraceful.
Stealing through politics
is not a sin at all;
selling justice for gain
is seen as social contract;
Slaughtering in war
so conquerors can boast
is power politics and glory;
Skinning poor folks alive
is an honorable deed,
defending rights of property;
hoodwinking a poor soul
is called the genius of truth.
Fucking alone
is deemed a sin!
Enlightened century, indeed!
A fucked up century!

A Li Decuriuni

Strati, teatri, orologi, campani,
Lazzaretti, Casini, Campi santi,
Licei, scoli normali, lancastriani,
Sunnu,di 'na citati li gran vanti.
E sirragghi, e mulini, e novi chiani,
Quatri, libra, e gran statui di rignanti...
Ma chi su?... si 'un pinsamu a li puttani,

Si 'un fabbricamu chiddi lochi santi?
Rispigghiativi, o gran decuriuna,
Nun mustrati chi siti senza cazzu,
Ma cchiù tostu ch'aviti li cugghiuna.
Faciti un locu 'nta Sicilia sulu,
Unni futtennu in comudu pagghiazzu
Lu cazzu scialirria 'nta sticchiu e culu.

A la Barunissa

Epigramma

La Signura Barunissa
Vinnia cara la sò fissa;
Perciò ditta fu l'avara
Barunissa fissa cara.

To Our Leaders

Avenues, theatres, belltowers, clocks
hospitals, cemeteries, and casinos;
Lyceums, vocational and grade schools
are things men prize in cities rightfully.
Also serraglios windmills and new squares,
paintings and books and kings' great statues...
But what are these if we don't think of whores,

if we do not erect those holy places?
You, leaders of our city, please wake up!
Don't show the world that you don't have a dick
but rather that you have a pair of balls.
In Sicily construct a place unique
where fucking on a cozy bed each dick
pussies and asses could then choose and pick.

To the Baroness

Epigram

Madam the Baroness
put a high price upon her pussy.
And for this, they named the hussy:
the "dear-pussy-Baroness."

Lu futtiri a volu

A Rusidda

Rusidda, si cchiù dura stu martiriu,
Ci lassu l'arma, ci appizzu lu coriu.
Sta ciamma chi mi porta a lu deliriu,
Mi trascina pi certu a lu martoriu,
Stu futtiri arrubbatu è ddu martiriu,
Chi nun si prova mancu in purgatoriu,
O fatu ffuttutissimu cuntrariu!
A volu t'haiu a futtiri 'ntra l'ariu!

Futti a volu lu passaru, e lu gaddu;
Futti a volu lu merru, e lu cardiddu;
Ma vidi comu futti lu cavaddu,
Chi un'ura si ci strica miatiddu!

Si 'ntra lu sticchiu nun ci fai lu caddu,
Si nun t'arriva 'ntra l'ossu pizziddu,
Si 'un ti lu scorciu tuttu, e 'un ti lu speddu,
Chi gustu ci avirrà ssu sticchiareddu?

Fucking on the Fly

To Rusidda

Rusidda, if this suffering goes on
I will give up the ghost and I'll be gone!
This loving flame that's driving me insane
will be the death of me, I know for sure!
This fucking on the fly is such a pain
no soul in Purgatory suffers more.
What fucked up destiny is mine to bear!
I've got to fuck you always on the fly!

Sparrows and roosters fuck high in the air,
black birds and cardinals will screw on high,
but look at how the horse enjoys his feast!
He lingers there an hour, blessed beast!

If from a pussy dicks don't get a callous,
if I do not sink deep with my big phallus,
if I don't wear it out and make it raw,
what kind of joy will your sweet pussy know?

Ottavi

Mi sentu forti strinciri lu cori:
'Na manu niura s'aggrava a lu pettu:
Ed una vuci lamintusa, mori,
Chi grida da dda fossa, eccu ti aspettu.
Ssi spassi, ssi grannizzi, ssi tesori
Da cà a un atomu! 'un hannu nuddu effettu,
E 'ntra st'abissu eternu di lu nenti,
Nenti sarrai tu puru eternamenti.

Sciala, mentri chi nn'hai, sciala ssu cori,
Mentri chi ancora sbatti 'ntra lu pettu;
Si speri autri piaciri, quannu mori,
Guarda a mia, comu ammatula l'aspettu?
Godi dunca ssi spassi, e ssi tesori,
Mentri chi puoi gustarni di l'effettu,
Godili tutti, 'unni lassari nenti,
Si li lassi li lassi eternamenti.

Futtemu dunca cu tuttu lu cori,
Strinciti, Lidda mia, pettu cu pettu.
'Unn'è cchiù morti si accussì si mori;
Cussì la vogghiu, la disiu, l'aspettu.
Su ssi biddizzi toi li mei tesori!
Di li piaciri mei causa ed effettu,
Si muremu futtennu, 'nn'è cchiù nenti
Morti, ma futtiremu eternamenti.

Octaves

I feel a heaviness around my chest:
a black hand's weighing heavy on my heart:
and from a grave a voice that sounds distressed
is saying "Die! I'm waiting here for you!"
Your pastimes and your splendors, all your treasures
will fade to dust! They count for nothing here,
and into this abyss of nothingness
you too will nothing be, eternally.

Amuse yourself, enjoy it while you can,
while your heart strongly beats inside your chest.
If you expect from death some other pleasures,
just look at me! See how I wait in vain.
Enjoy therefore your pastimes and your treasures,
while you can feel the joys that they contain.
Enjoy them all don't leave a thing behind!
For if you do, there's nothing else to find.

So let us screw then with our heart of hearts.
Hold tight, my Lidda, breast against my breast.
Dying like this would be no death at all.
That's how I want it, that's how death should be.
Your beauties are my treasures and my joys:
cause and effect of all that pleases me.
If death should overtake us as we screw,
death would be nothing. I'd keep fucking you.

La Svirginatura

Lici, e lu 'nnamuratu

Sonettu I

"Ahi! ahi!... chistu ch'è modu?... lu dicia...
Tradituri, mi vasi, e poi m'ammazzi?...
Ahi! ahi!... sinu a stu signu!... 'un ci cridia!
Darmi stu corpu mentri chi m'abbrazzi?...
Ddoppu di tantu amuri... 'un suppunia!...
Ma tutti tutti cani st'uminazzi!...
Vidi?... hai fattu ssa bella vapparia...
Ma nui fimmini, nui semu li pazzi.
Pri chissu mi dicivi: un fari vuci
E appuiannula poi peiu di peiu
'Mpunta mi la trasivi duci duci?
Tuttu 'nta un corpu quantu mi firisti...
Pi avirlu sanu hai fattu tantu preu,
Ora dunca pirchì mi lu rumpisti?..."

Sonettu II

"No, nun ti lu rumpivi, gioja mia!
Ma grapennu la porta a lu piaciri,
Pruvirrai quali gustu t'arricria,
Gustu, ch'avirrai cosi di 'nfuddiri.
Eu fari un mali? fari un mali a tia?...
Centu voti vurria megghiu muriri.
Dah levatillu da la fantasia,
M'ammazza ssu to chiantu, e ssi suspiri!
Arma di l'arma mia, facemu paci.
Pruvamu nautra vota, e vidirrai...
Ti moru ccà davanti, si 'un ti piaci.
Lu vosi sanu, pr'essiri sicuru,
Chi cu lu primu coppu tanti guai
Arrimuddavi ssu to cori duru".

The Deflowering

Lici and Her Lover

Sonnet I

Ahi! Ahi! Is that the way you act? I knew it!
You traitor, first you kiss and then you slay me!
Ahi! ahi! I never dreamed it possible that you,
while hugging me, would strike me in such way!
After I loved you so...I never thought !
Ah men!.. What rotten loathsome swines they are!
You should be proud indeed! Look what you've
                                            wrought!
We women are the ones who are insane!
That's why you kept repeating, "Don't scream, dear!"
And then proceeding slowly, bye and bye,
you penetrated me without much haste.
But then you wounded me with that sharp thrust.
You made such a great fuss to have it whole!
Why then did you proceed to break my hole?"

Sonnet II

"Oh no, I didn't break it, life of mine!
but now that I have opened pleasure's main,
you're free to savor joys that are divine,
such pleasure that will drive you quite insane.
Me hurting anyone? Me hurting you?
I would have died a hundred deaths before!
Just drive the thought out of your head, please do!
Your tears and sighs are more than I can bear.
Breath of my life, let's make peace, instead.
Let's try once more, you'll like it fine...I swear!
And if you don't, I promise to drop dead!
I wanted it intact so I'd be sure
that after all my woes I'd be the one
who'd soften your unyielding heart of stone."

Sonnet III

"'Nsaiamu, Lici mia, daja 'nsaiamu.
La nesciu appena appena dici ahi ahi.
Dunca nun l'hai pruvatu si gheu t'amu?
Pi tia stissa lu fazzu, e nun lu sai.
Vasami... ancugna... vasami... vasamu.
Un momentu". "Arma mia chi cosa fai?..."
"Ch'è fari si ti torci comu n'amu.
Curuzzu, e comu puoi gustarla mai?...
Sta soda... vasa... abbrazza forti... strinci...
Accussì... nun ti moviri, e t'aisu
Ssi naticheddi... ssu culiddu spinci...
Accussì... tremi... dà... vasami... vasa...
Ti veni?..." "Ciatu meu!.. chi Paradisu!..
Arma di l'arma mia!... 'ncasala! 'ncasa!..."

Lu pinitenti doppu la missioni

E chi ci aisi, minchia mia, ssa testa?
Dunca 'un lu senti chi a' campari casta?
Ci cridi chi c'è 'nfernu?... e ancora o pesta!
Lu panuzzu di casa nun t'abbasta?
'N'ucchiata appena, ed eccuti già lesta:
'Na 'mmistuta, e si dura comu un'asta:
Vidi 'na scialla, 'na fodedda, o vesta
Nnarmalisci, e 'nc'è causi chi ci basta.
Mischina mia! chi mi 'ntuppasti trista!
A farimi dannari è fatta apposta.
'Un c'è rimediu si 'un mi levu a chista?
Sai però chi ti dicu; si mi susta,
Ssi dui vappi pi cui si tanta tosta
Zaffi... e l'appennu in vutu pi cchiù frusta.

Sonnet III

"Lici, let's try again! Come on, let try!
I'll pull it out the moment you say ahi!
Haven't I proved that for your love I'd die?
I'm doing it for you, that is no lie.
So kiss me, hug me, oh let's kiss again.
Hold on!" "What are you doing, now, my love?"
"You're wriggling like a worm! How can I gain
a hold...how can you savor it, by Jove?
Embrace me now, stay still, give me a kiss,
like so! Don't move now so that I can raise
your little thighs! Push up with your sweet ass!
Like that! You're trembling, kiss me more, oh please!
You're coming?" "It's paradise, soul of my soul,
What joy! Oh, plunge it deeper in my hole!"

The Penitent After Confession

I say, my cock, why do you raise your head?
Haven't you heard that you must now be chaste?
Don't you believe in hell? The homemade bread
is not enough for you, you shameless pest!
A glance is all you need and you're impressed;
a bump and you are quickly hard and bold;
a shawl, a slip, a dress, and you're obsessed,
a beast! Pants cannot keep you in their hold.
Poor me! What scoundrel you turned out to be!
To damn my soul, that is why you exist!
With you around, can there be remedy?
But listen carefully! If you persist,
see those two machos whence you get your gall?
One snip...for spite! I'll hang them on the wall!

La rosa e lu poeta Simuncelli
cu lu nasu fradiciu

Poeta

"Dunca si t'avi a cogghiri
'Na manu e cu si sia,
Dunca pirchì 'un pò essiri
Chista la manu mia?"

Rosa

Su fatta pi lu ciauru:
E comu mai putria
Ssu nasu e cazzu maghiru
Priarisi di mia?

Poeta

Sì rosa, e nun sì rosa:
Leva l'allegoria,
Sì Nici, e comu fimmina
Chi mali ci sarria?

Rosa

Rispunnu comu fimmina:
La nostra fantasia
Lu stasu pri conusciri
Lu nasu si talia.
Dunca cu chissu strummalu,
Ss'orribili sfrinzia,
O fussi Rosa o fimmina
Chi cazzu vuoi di mia?

The Rose and the Poet Simuncelli
with a Rotten Nose

Poet

Please tell me, if you're free
for any man at all
to gather you at will
why can't that man be me?

Rose

The sense of smell I please.
So then how could a nose
and puny cock like yours
take pleasures from a rose?

Poet

A rose you are and aren't.
Let allegories be!
You're Nici and as woman
what find you wrong with me?

Rose

As woman I'll reply:
when women fantasize
to know a cock's true size
the nose they analyze
Therefore, with such a nose,
a wee monstrosity,
were I a girl or rose,
what could you want from me?

Lu 'nglisi o sia la metempsicosi

Su già sunati quarantaquattr'anni
La scala ch'acchianai prestu si scinni;
S'accosta la vicchizza e li malanni
E la morti mi grida: venitinni:
Li Bacici?... li Lici?... li Giuvanni?...
Addiu culi, addiu sticchi, ed addiu minni
Però un pinseri mi fa cori granni,
Chi ti nni 'mporta un cazzu, futtitinni!
Si rinasciu, cusà nasciu stadduni?
E sarogghiu di futtiri cchiù liccu
Cu di gran cugghiunazza appinnuluni.
E cui lu sapi si rinasciu beccu?
E cu lu sapi si rinasciu miccu?
Però pi minchia, mi cuntentu sceccu.

The English or Reincarnation

I am already forty-four years old.
The ladder going down is quickly paced.
Old age and troubles are quickfooted, bold
and death is beckoning to me: "Make haste!"
What of the Fannies, Licis and the Jocks?
Farewell, sweet asses, pussies, teats godbye!
But something's on my mind. What if my cock...
Forget it! Thoughts like that don't dignify!
But what if I'm reborn, say, as a stud,
a stallion hornier than anything
with a great pair of balls that hang and swing?
What if my dick's a total loss, a dud?
What if I am reborn as a hegoat?
A donkey's rod would be, though, a nice thought!

Li cugghiuna

C'è da taluni ferma opinioni
da taluni si cridi idea chimerica
se i coglioni entran mai nell'azioni
dintra la fissa, non essennu sferica.
Eccu propongu a lei la quistioni,
a Lei Poeta cu tanta di cherica.
Figliu miu, mi metti in consternazioni,
la quistioni, o figliu, è climaterica.
Per me, riguardu a fisica 'un m'intricu;
ma pi l'esperienza di tant'anni
li cugghiuna 'un trasianu 'ntempu anticu.
Ora però sia sticchiu nicu o granni
sfunnuranu macari lu biddicu:
ora un cugghiuni trasi a tutti banni.

The Testicles

Some of the people hold it to be true,
others believe that it's fantastical
to think that testicles can penetrate
a pussy, since it is not spherical.
I'd like to pose the question now to you,
a poet whose great laurels are not few.
Your query throws me deep in consternation
because, my son, it deals with acclimation.
As for the physics, I've no explanation.
But in my many years of observation,
I never knew them to go in before.
Now testicles drive deep into the core,
be pussies tight or wide as thoroughfares:
nowadays a testicle* goes everywhere!

"Cugghiuni" in Sicilian has several meanings, which
correspond with the English terms "dickhead, asshole,
moron". The last line plays on this "double entendre."